Anna Maria College: 1946 - 1996

A Mission Evolves

Anna Maria College:
1946 - 1996

A Mission Evolves

By Bernadette Madore, S.S.A., Ph.D.

Ambassador Books • Worcester, Massachusetts

ISBN: 1-929039-03-4
Library of Congress Catalog Card Number: 00-104308

Published in the United States by Ambassador Books, Inc.
71 Elm Street, Worcester, Massachusetts 01609
(800) 577-0909

Printed in Canada.

DEDICATION

*To Sister Pauline Madore, S.S.A., '62
and to all our alumni who have gone forward
to enjoy the fruits of their education
and who are the voice of the college in all walks of life.
Anna Maria College is grateful to each one.
To those who have preceded us in Life we say:
be our intercessors before the throne of God.*

TABLE OF CONTENTS

ACKNOWLEDGMENTS

In retrospect, the evolution of the mission of Anna Maria College was a dynamic process which insured the vitality of its growth. It was my wish to describe the development of this mission so inextricably woven into the fabric of Anna Maria College through the first fifty years of its existence. Having spent most of my professional life at the college and having been part of its growth from 1947 to the present, it was an exciting project to undertake and bring to fruition. My successor in the presidency, Sister Rita Larivee, S.S.A., commissioned me early in her tenure to write the fifty-year history of the college. The trustees, at that time, supported her request. Her unfailing encouragement and that of former president Sister Irene Socquet were very important to me.

Describing this evolution, however, required intense and detailed research of events, people, and times. Reports written and addressed to the campus community, the president, or the board of trustees, during my tenure as dean or president support the factual dimensions of this work as do the reports of two former presidents, one by Sister Caroline Finn and several by Sister Irene Socquet. In addition, letters written to the alumni in their various publications such as *Milestone* also enabled the chronicling of events over the years.

The archives at the mother house and at St. Marie provincial house of the Sisters of Saint Anne yielded some interesting facts, especially those regarding the events surrounding the foundation of the college and the early implementation of its mission. The yearly chronicles written by the Sisters of Saint Anne living on campus also have been a rich source of information. The wealth of detail in these chronicles reveals the ethos of the college created by the living out of the mission in the pioneer years. The minutes of the meetings of the corporation, *The Sisters of St. Ann*, are filled with precise data. [This is the title of the corporation. It is not to be confused with the name of the congregation: The Sisters of Saint Anne.] The photos are the property of the college or of the author. Most of them, in time, will be found in the AMC archives, in Paxton. I hereby acknowledge these important sources and am especially grateful to the archivists at the mother house and the provincial house who were most gracious in assisting me.

Dr. Bernard Parker, president of AMC (1996-99), introduced me to his friend Dr. James

Horgan, author of the history of St. Leo College, who provided very valuable advice. I am grateful to him and to Dr. Parker. It was my good fortune to have Sister Patricia Fontaine, S.S.A., Ph.D., edit the chapters of the first draft of the document. I am very much in her debt for her patience and moral support. My friend, Kenneth F. Black, also read the chapters with a view to keeping me focused on the expression and evolution of the mission of the college. His was a constant reminder of viewing the alumni as living heralds of this mission and of its contribution in their lives. I thank him for his wisdom and moral support. Dr. Paul Russell, chairperson of the history and political science department of Anna Maria College, accompanied me especially through the second draft of the manuscript, diligently edited every chapter, and made important suggestions. I am grateful to him. My gratitude extends to those who read and commented on the manuscript, especially Dr. Charles Hepburn, historian, and former vice-president of Anna Maria College. To the alumni, faculty, and friends for contributing vignettes that add an interesting element of diversion to the text, I am deeply grateful. I thank the provincial leaders of St. Marie Province for their interest and caring. For her timely advocacy and support, I am grateful to Sister Paulette Gardner, S.S.A., chairperson of the board of trustees. The final impetus making the publication of the manuscript a reality came from President William D. McGarry (1999 —). I am in his debt. The value and importance of having *Ambassador Books, Inc.* publish the manuscript cannot be overestimated. Both Gerard and Jennifer Goggins left no stone unturned to insure that the finished product would be of the highest quality. They know how to achieve excellence. In addition, their patience, resourcefulness, creativity, and attention to details are deep-seated characteristics which can hardly be overlooked by the listener or the observer. They were never too busy to listen, suggest, and make recommendations leading to high quality results. I am grateful to both of them.

The book describes, from a collaborative perspective, the way events were perceived and experienced. Sources and authors have been conscientiously acknowledged. The purpose of the work is to acquaint friends, students, and others of the broader community with the development of what is known as Anna Maria College. Much more could have been written, but to speed the readers on their way to a knowledge of AMC, it was important not to divert attention from the flow of the text by too many interesting but perhaps nonessential details. However, the vignettes which carry the words of other members of the college community throughout its history do add an anecdotal dimension to the work.

— *Sister Bernadette Madore, S.S.A.*

"To elevate the heart through love,
To enlighten the intellect in truth,
To strengthen the will in good."

— Anna Maria College 1948-1949 catalog

I

ORIGINS

On September 8, 1850, in the parish church of Vaudreuil, in the Canadian province of Quebec, Esther Blondin and four companions pronounced religious vows. At that time, in the middle of the nineteenth century, there was a tremendous void to be filled in the field of education because illiteracy was rampant in the small villages and farmlands of French Canadian Quebec. Esther had recruited her four companions to fulfill a longtime dream—to empower people, especially the poor, illiterate children of the Quebec countryside, by teaching them religion, reading, writing, and arithmetic. With great audacity and courage, Esther, now called Mother Marie Anne, pursued her vision and translated it into the remarkable teaching mission of the Sisters of Saint Anne, the congregation which she founded 150 years ago. The ranks of Mother Marie Anne's little community swelled, and in time her daughters could be found in North and South America, the West

Blondin Academy, Vaudreuil, Quebec.

Indies, and in the Cameroon, Africa. Before World War II, they also served in Japan.[1]

In 1867, the Sisters of Saint Anne opened their first school in the United States and quickly extended their field of action to the archdiocese of Boston, as well as to the dioceses of Providence, Albany, and Springfield. However, the year 1887 was particularly significant for Anna Maria

College, for it was then that the congregation was incorporated in the Commonwealth of Massachusetts. The new charter facilitated loans for the construction of St. Anne Academy, which opened in 1888 in Marlboro, MA. It was that very charter which fifty-nine years later, in 1946, made it possible for the corporation, *The Sisters of St. Ann*, to receive degree-granting powers for Anna Maria College.[2]

The mission which was articulated by Mother Marie Anne, when she founded the Congregation of the Sisters of Saint Anne, has retained its meaning and power ever since and has been the guiding force for those who choose to follow her way of life. In our times, as in decades past, these women attempt to fill unmet needs in society by responding to the prompting of the Spirit. Hospitals, boarding schools, day schools, clinics, and other works of mercy are all tributes to the desire of the Sisters of Saint Anne to fill these perceived wants. Today's Sisters of Saint Anne, like Esther Blondin, open their eyes and hearts to contemporary needs. Like Esther, they sometimes face distrust and opposition; for visions are by nature upsetting especially when they lead through uncharted waters and unmapped territories. Visionaries are seldom understood. If not always admired, they are certainly noticed because, as movers and shakers, they tend to upset the *status quo*.

Mother house of the Sisters of Saint Anne, Lachine, Quebec.

If it were not for Esther Blondin and the visionaries who followed her and dared to dream great dreams, there would be no Anna Maria College. It was with a deep sense of mission and great faith that Sister M. Anne Eva Mondor and her companions overcame many difficulties to open the college in 1946. [Most of the religious names of the sisters included the name Marie, hence the capital M after the word sister.] Their mission was to educate in the most complete sense of the word—not merely by the communication of knowledge, but by the development and enhancement of moral, intellectual, and spiritual values as well. The mission stated in the 1948-1949 catalog is an excellent summation of that ideal:

Anna Maria College offers a liberal education planned:

> *to elevate the heart through love,*
> *to enlighten the intellect in truth,*
> *to strengthen the will in good.*[3]

A set of guiding principles provided the dynamism needed to accomplish this mission. These principles, which were nurtured by the Catholic presence of the sisters, created an ethos which gave the college its special character. The same concern for the poor, which animated Esther, inspired the Sisters of Saint Anne who founded Anna Maria College. Their goal was to make higher education available to women of modest means. They kept tuition affordable thereby empowering middle-class families to meet the costs of a college education for their promising daughters. In time, Anna Maria College's mission was expanded to include men. Later still, that mission grew to include working men and women, providing them with an education which offered the opportunity for career mobility and change. The founding of Anna Maria College was a step forward in the evolution of Esther Blondin's initial mission favoring the very poor. The mission now included teaching and empowering the working class, the middle class, and all men and women of any class in need of higher education.

The establishment of Anna Maria College in Paxton required courage in all of its dimensions, dedication, and constant hard work. It demonstrated the visionary ideal of the founding members—passed on to a large number of colleagues, lay and religious—as well as the caring and gratitude of alumni, and the support and generosity of loyal friends.

*"Send your superiors to me and
I shall see what I can do."*

— Archbishop Cushing

II

AN AMERICAN COLLEGE: A DREAM AND A VISION

Anna Maria College and its mission were the fruit of a dream and a vision. Imagine living in the decade of the forties—the world was at war—but on the home front, in Marlboro Massachusetts, a Sister of Saint Anne, Sister M. Rose Isabel (Eagen), senior class teacher at St. Anne Academy, was assisting her students, as she had done for several years, in choosing colleges best suited for those in search of a baccalaureate degree. All the while, she and her colleagues wished for the day when there would be a college under the auspices of the Sisters of Saint Anne on American soil.

The Sisters of Saint Anne already directed a college in Montreal, Canada, known as *College Marie-Anne*.[4] It had two sections—one for French-Canadian students, and another, where courses were offered in English to English-speaking students, most of whom were American women. The Sisters of Saint Anne who taught in the English section were also committed to the vision of a college on American soil. They even

projected that the large high schools staffed by their religious order would be fertile ground for recruiting college students. The dream and the vision became so clear that, at the General Chapter of 1943, a request was made that the Sisters of Saint Anne found a college in the United States.[5] The General Chapter entrusted the implementation of this decision to the General Council consisting of the general superior and her councillors.

In May 1945, Archbishop Cushing, metropolitan of the archdiocese of Boston, came to St. Mary Church in Marlboro for confirmation ceremonies. As was customary, he was invited to meet the students of St. Anne Academy in their auditorium. Touched by words of welcome delivered by one of the seniors, he invited the senior class and their teachers to visit him at his residence in Brighton. The students were overjoyed. Thus, early in June 1945, Sister M. Rose Isabel, the senior class teacher, accompanied the members of the class on their visit to the residence of Archbishop Cushing. The archbishop

THE SISTERS OF SAINT ANNE

*A*ll the sisters were exceptionally well-educated and young although we did not realize the latter when we were in their charge. By their example they inspired us to do our best (they expected our best to be really the best). From the very beginning we knew that as young women we were every bit as intelligent and scholarly as any of the male students in other area colleges. Always we were encouraged to seek, to strive, to earn our places in the world, to make purposeful contributions to our communities and to our world. These same educated, spiritual women spent their "free" time doing research and earning more advanced degrees. What salaries they earned were turned back to the college so that we would be the beneficiaries of a free, Catholic education. They were determined to pass on their love of learning and their standards to us so that we in turn would pass on the traditions to a new generation.

— Carol Harding, Class of 1955

was lavish with his time, conducted a tour through his residence, including his own room (casual as the archbishop himself) and, in the late afternoon, offered Benediction in his private chapel. Sister M. Rose Isabel, in thanking him for this unusual privilege, asked: "If my congregation wished to found a liberal arts college in your archdiocese, would it have your blessing?" It was a very warm day and while the archbishop wiped perspiration from his face, he seemed not only surprised but also pleased. He answered by saying, "Send your superiors to me and I shall see what I can do."

Again in June 1945, Sister M. Rose Isabel accompanied a group of students to Montreal where Daniel J. Lord, S. J., was holding his annual Summer School of Catholic Action. She and her students had accommodations at *College Marie-Anne*, on 12th Avenue, Lachine. Every day, Sister M. Rose Isabel met Sister M. Anne Eva, directress of studies, who resided at the

mother house close by. Sister M. Rose Isabel shared with her the conversation she had had with Archbishop Cushing regarding the opening of a college in his archdiocese. She hoped that Sister M. Anne Eva, whose dream was also for a new college, would carry the message to Mother M. Leopoldine, the general superior. Sister M. Anne Eva seemed reticent and suggested that Sister M. Rose Isabel herself inform Mother M. Leopoldine. After the sessions of the next day, Sister M. Rose Isabel rode to the mother house in the hope of seeing the general superior. It was five o'clock and the sisters, including Mother M. Leopoldine, were leaving the chapel after Benediction. Sister M. Rose Isabel met the general superior as she reached the foot of the stairs on her way to her office. She asked for a few minutes of conversation. Mother M. Leopoldine hesitated saying that she was in a great hurry— because she was leaving the next day for Marlboro. Sister M. Rose Isabel, undaunted, pleaded for a few minutes of the general superior's time. The latter reluctantly acquiesced, though she did not invite her to her office, a short distance away on the same floor, but stepped into a small room nearby and remained standing while listening to Sister M. Rose Isabel's account of her conversation with Archbishop Cushing. Much to Sister M. Rose Isabel's pleasant surprise, Mother M. Leopoldine showed great interest. She even wondered out loud who would accompany her to meet with the archbishop should he grant her an interview. Sister M. Rose Isabel suggested that the directress of studies, Sister M. Anne Eva, should be the one to accompany Mother M. Leopoldine. She offered to make the necessary contacts. Sister M. Anne Eva accepted and agreed to leave the next morning for Marlboro as a companion to the general superior.

In her unpublished notes,[6] Sister M. Rose Isabel related the details given to her by Sister M. Anne Eva who was present at the meeting between Archbishop Cushing and Mother M. Leopoldine on July 2, 1945. How fascinating but unlike were the personalities of the two main players involved in this interview! Mother M. Leopoldine, an American citizen, was tall, stately, dignified, and very much a lady in the Victorian tradition and had served for many years as general superior of the Sisters of Saint Anne. She was respected and admired by all the bishops in the Province of Quebec. Mother M. Leopoldine and Sister M. Anne Eva, who accompanied her to visit the archbishop, waited for Archbishop Cushing in the main parlor of his residence in Brighton. He breezed in promptly and, in his customary casual and friendly manner, said: "Hi there, Sisters. How are you?" Mother M. Leopoldine was rather stunned at his lack of decorum. She had never met a member of the episcopacy quite like him! A true son of South Boston, he was earthy, friendly, and quick to speak his mind. On this occasion, the archbishop praised the work done in his archdiocese by the Sisters of Saint Anne. He expressed great delight that they were considering founding a

college and assured them of his interest and assistance. He suggested that they contact Father Timothy F. O'Leary, superintendent of Catholic Schools in the Boston archdiocese.

After her visit with Archbishop Cushing, Mother M. Leopoldine spent some time with the sisters at Saint Anne Academy in Marlboro. Just before her return to the mother house, she called for a general assembly of the American Province of the Sisters of Saint Anne, comprising 379 sisters dispersed in twenty convents in the northeast. The main purpose of the assembly was to announce that the congregation was considering founding a liberal arts college in the Boston archdiocese.

To prepare the groundwork for a new college, Sister M. Anne Eva was formally appointed in charge of all plans for this project. She spent the rest of the summer and the fall months of 1945 at St. Anne Academy in Marlboro. Not long after assuming her new duties, Sister M. Anne Eva wrote to the general superior about her first

A CHRISTIAN EDUCATION

*Robert J. Lemieux
in the sixties*

*T*here is no real substitute for the Christian liberal arts college. The burden, both pedagogical and financial, will always be a heavy one. But learning the arts and sciences as neutral towards God effectively separates them from an authentic Christian life. The result of such an education is not a Christian person but someone who—reflecting perhaps his or her neutral curricular experience—is four-fifths neutral and, at most, one-fifth committed to the Christian life.

...The arts and sciences are good. All of them. And, as we say in some of our classes, they are good "in themselves." By this we mean that they are worth pursuing, for themselves, because they are truly perfective of us as human beings. But they are not good enough for a Christian unless they come to exist within the ambit of his or her love of God.

An authentic Christian education is a total one. At Anna Maria, we seek not just the knowledge of the arts and sciences, but also the mystery that surrounds them. And we can settle for nothing less than all of reality, whole and entire, visible and invisible. This is our legacy and we have no other.

No one, perhaps, has summed it up better than the French Renaissance writer and naughty monk Francois Rabelais: "Sciences without conscience is but the ruin of the soul."

—*Robert J. Lemieux, Professor of philosophy and French*

meeting with Father O'Leary whom Archbishop Cushing had assigned to be her mentor. Excerpts of her letter follow:[7]

...I have had my first interview with Father Timothy O'Leary with the result that I am beginning to know where we stand. Father is a very fine young priest, thirty-eight years of age, very keen of intellect, quick of perception and very sympathetic and understanding. My impression is that the most reverend archbishop was right when he referred me to him, and under his direction I feel confident already that there will be no difficulty whatsoever about procuring a charter.

Not only does he intend to get state authorization to grant the degrees I mentioned but he will make the request comprehensive enough to include all higher degrees, so that in later years if we have the faculty for it these degrees can be granted. He told me that he would employ the services of an eminent lawyer whom he knows...because of his relations with him at the Catholic University of America and, with him as our advocate, there will be no trouble at all about obtaining the charter....

The "eminent lawyer" was Attorney Joseph C. Duggan, assistant to the attorney general of the United States, in New Bedford.

With the help of Sister M. Rose Isabel, who over many years had established a network of influential friends, Sister M. Anne Eva made solid contacts with people who would be her supporters in the legislature. In her memoirs, Sister M. Rose Isabel wrote that one of her former students, Eleanor Byrne, had married Norman Wellen, who had been recently elected to the Massachusetts House of Representatives. Mr. Wellen would be greatly instrumental in making the project known in the legislature where votes were important. As part of her man-

date, Sister M. Anne Eva was also in touch with Dr. Roy Deferrari, secretary general of the Catholic University of America and chairman of the American Association of Accredited Colleges and Universities. As chairman of the latter association, he was called upon to travel across the country to assist, advise, and review accredited colleges and universities. In addition, the secretary sponsored and directed an affiliation program with Catholic colleges to assist them in meeting the demands of higher education in their various states. He was not only familiar with the essential conditions for the proper functioning of a college, but he was also aware of the many pitfalls which awaited the uninitiated. He was one of the most prominent figures at educational conventions and was highly respected.

On October 4, 1945, Sister M. Anne Eva wrote as follows to Dr. Roy Deferrari:[8]

We, the Sisters of Saint Anne, have requested and obtained the permission of His Excellency, Richard J. Cushing, archbishop of Boston, to open a college in Marlboro, Mass.

In the course of an interview I had yesterday with Reverend Timothy F. O'Leary to whom his excellency had referred me for direction, Father suggested that, in order to have the best guarantee of judicious planning, we should have recourse to your authoritative guidance and invite you to Marlboro, where we could talk the matter over with you. Father O'Leary promised to be here also to meet you.

I have come from Montreal to Marlboro for the purpose of obtaining a state charter. My stay here cannot be prolonged indefinitely, yet I do not care to carry on any legal proceedings before I know definitively from you whether or not our venture is a wise one and on what conditions its success will depend.

*Clockwise from top left: Dr. Roy J. Deferrari (on left), Archbishop Richard J. Cushing,
Reverend Timothy F. O'Leary, Attorney Joseph C. Duggan.*

The purpose of this letter then is to invite you most cordially to St. Anne Academy where an enthusiastic welcome awaits you.

Dr. Deferrari came to Marlboro on November 2, 1945, and had lengthy discussions with Sister M. Anne Eva and her advisor, Father O'Leary. He encouraged both of them to open the college as soon as possible and to select a well-prepared faculty. He stated that no accrediting agency would review the college until the charter class had graduated, and thus Sister M. Anne Eva had four years to prepare a highly qualified faculty. To her lasting credit she did just that. She scrutinized the aptitudes of the teaching personnel of the congregation both in Montreal and in New England and obtained authorization to send a few promising young sisters to the Catholic University of America. Her correspondence with the general superior demonstrated her understanding of the value of a well-prepared faculty and her determination

to obtain the proper training for chosen candidates.

Sister M. Anne Eva realized that Dr. Deferrari, a staunch Catholic, protected the interests of Catholic institutions and she placed her trust in his unparalleled ability. She supplied him with all the information he required about the nascent college in order to warrant a one-year affiliation with the Catholic University of America (CUA). Five months after Dr. Deferrari's visit, Sister M. Anne Eva received the following letter:[9]

...At a recent meeting of the Academic Senate, the affiliation of Anna Maria College, Marlboro, Massachusetts, as a senior college for a one-year period, was approved. This was done on the recommendation of the Committee on Affiliation.

The Committee recommended that at the end of the first year a questionnaire be

---

STUDYING AT ANNA MARIA COLLEGE

*I*n 1946, I witnessed the launching of a brave new college in Marlboro, Massachusetts. Later as a student, staff, and faculty member, I marveled at Anna Maria College's ability to survive and prosper. I wondered what secret force enabled the institution to grow when so many others plummeted. I recognized a spirit in the pioneer sisters energized by a prayer life, an affinity for hard work, a commitment to excellence—all tempered by a sense of humor.

For several years, I was among the bus-load of sisters from Canada who invaded the Paxton campus each summer in search of a solid education. We knew we were in for six weeks of hard work but we also anticipated joyful reunions of friends and a sharing of the past year's events, happy as well as sad. Our hard-working teachers (sometimes regarded as benevolent slave-drivers) kept us busy, not only in the classroom but also in the library, the botanical paths, and the laboratories. In addition, the Cournoyer farm adjoined the campus—and we responded to the generous owner who offered the college anything that could be picked from the fields.

Back to Canada, our six-week experience provided innumerable stories to be narrated on many occasions during the seclusion of long Canadian winters. At Anna Maria College, we received more than higher education—opportunities abounded to grow in our community spirit of dedication and generosity. It was all worthwhile!

— *Patricia Fontaine, S.S.A., Ph.D., Class of 1961*

filled out and that another inspection be made at that time....Within a short time you will also receive a certificate of your affiliation with the University.

Some twenty days later she informed Father O'Leary that she had received the Certificate of Affiliation with the Catholic University of America.

In the late fall of 1945, Father O'Leary real-ized that the Massachusetts Legislature enter-tained biennial sessions only and the next session would be held in January 1947. Both he and Sister M. Anne Eva had their hearts set on open-ing the college in September 1946. Father O'Leary invoked his close personal friendship with Governor Maurice J. Tobin who mandated a special session of the legislature for 1946 when the request for the charter would be considered. Their hopes soared!

"I am very happy to grant permission to the Sisters of Saint Anne to open a college of liberal arts in Marlboro, Massachusetts."

— Archbishop Cushing

III

CHARTERING A COLLEGE

Together, Sister M. Anne Eva, Father O'Leary, and Attorney Duggan drafted a petition to the Massachusetts Board of Collegiate Authority. The purpose was to obtain an amendment to the Incorporation Act of July 14, 1887, which would extend the powers of the corporation, *The Sisters of St. Ann*, so that it could establish an institution for the higher education of women in Marlboro, Massachusetts with the right to confer all degrees usually conferred by such institutions in the Commonwealth of Massachusetts, except medical degrees and the degree of bachelor of laws.

To support their petition, Sister M. Anne Eva supplied details concerning important matters, such as, the physical property of the projected institution, the stability of the organization, the nature of the other establishments directed by the Congregation of the Sisters of Saint Anne, the members of the corporation and their residence, endowments, tax-exemption, library, faculty, officers of administration, tuition, require-

ments for admission, requirements for graduation, and financial organization of the corporation: *The Sisters of St. Ann*.

Father O'Leary, in his letter of November 13, 1945, to Sister M. Anne Eva, added an interesting note regarding honorary degrees. "Mr. Joseph Duggan...has assured me that the power to grant honorary degrees to men and women is included in the bill...." In another letter written on December 4, 1945, Father O'Leary advised Sister M. Ann Eva:[10]

...In regard to the state representatives who are friends of the academy, I think it proper and wise to invite them jointly to sponsor the proposed legislation empowering the community to establish a college. I am enclosing Mr. Duggan's suggestions, therefore, in this connection, and I earnestly advise you and the representatives to follow his advice....Please arrange, therefore, as soon as possible to have the representatives

23

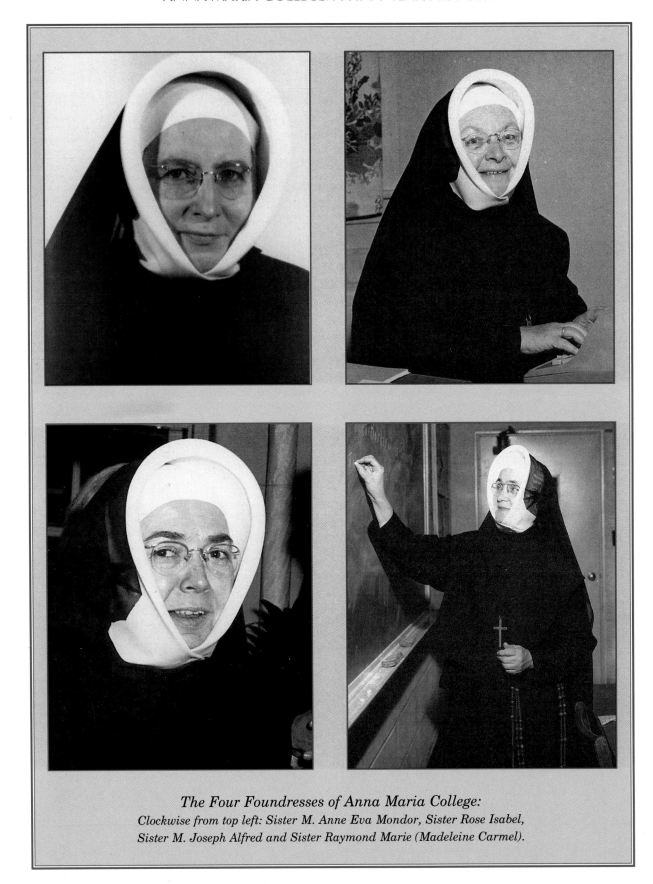

The Four Foundresses of Anna Maria College:
Clockwise from top left: Sister M. Anne Eva Mondor, Sister Rose Isabel,
Sister M. Joseph Alfred and Sister Raymond Marie (Madeleine Carmel).

coached by Mr. Duggan and to be ready for obtaining the necessary legislative action after January 1, 1946.

...May I suggest that you draw up a tentative circular advertising the opening of the college, the proposed curricula for obtaining the various degrees, and the plans for the physical structure of the institution?...No circulars, however, ought to be published until you are able to state the exact date of approval by the legislature. This will be forthcoming, so do not become worried.

Sister M. Anne Eva responded to Father O'Leary on December 17, 1945:[11]

...I want you to know that Mr. Norman Wellen, the representative of the District of Marlborough, has accepted to introduce the Bill for our proposed college at the next session of the legislature and to sponsor it for us. Mr. Ernest DeRoy of Chicopee will sign the Bill and will sponsor it with Mr. Wellen. These gentlemen met here on Saturday, December 15, and, as you directed, they will go to Boston shortly to be coached by Mr. Duggan....While visiting in Worcester last week, I contacted a few other members of the General Court, and all were very gracious and promised to favor the proposed legislation....

The stage was set—the project was taking shape—but other details needed attention. One of these was that the new college had to be formally authorized both by the congregation and by the archbishop of Boston. On January 5, 1946, the general council of the congregation met in a regular assembly and an agenda item specified the need to follow through on the authorization given by the general chapter of 1943 (in article 13) to open a liberal arts college for women in Marlboro, Massachusetts. The general council voted to found an American college in Marlboro, in the archdiocese of Boston. Even the name was discussed and that of *Anna Maria College* was chosen.

In her personal notes, Sister M. Rose Isabel wrote that Dr. Deferrari had counseled against choosing the name of a saint for the new college, to avoid prejudice—this final name was selected because it could easily be said in both English and French. The general council, at this point, was acting upon the verbal authorization of Archbishop Cushing given on July 2, 1945. The congregation needed written approval, and on January 24, 1946, Mother M. Leopoldine, general superior, dispatched the following letter to Archbishop Cushing:[12]

In the beginning of July 1945, your Excellency very kindly favored us with an interview at the archiepiscopal residence, during which you graciously authorized us to open a college of liberal arts in the city of Marlboro, Massachusetts.

In the course of our conversation, your Excellency referred us to the Reverend Timothy F. O'Leary, Ph.D., for guidance. It was under his very efficient and sympathetic direction that, through representative Norman Wellen, we presented to the legislature of the State of Massachusetts a bill requesting a charter that would empower our community to establish a college.

Before the members of the General Court bring to an end the necessary legislative action, we wish, in a more official manner, to solicit confirmation of your Excellency's approval of our proposed college and your blessing on so weighty an undertaking.

Permit us to express our sincere appreciation and gratitude for the paternal solicitude and kindly interest with which your Excellency favors our community.

On February 1, 1946, during a session of the general council, a letter, dated January 26, 1946, from Archbishop Cushing to the General Superior, Mother M. Leopoldine, was read to the members of the council, giving the written approval of the archbishop for the founding of the new college:[13]

I am very happy to grant permission to the Sisters of Saint Anne to open a college of liberal arts in Marlboro, Mass. I beg to give the project every blessing and the promise of many prayerful mementos.

At a later date I would like to meet the sisters who will be in charge of the institution. The prospect of the institution has already occasioned much favorable comment. In order that such comments might be turned into practical support, I would like to have one or two of the sisters who will be identified with the college call to see me at their earliest convenience.

After these formal actions were taken, the general superior traveled from Lachine to Marlboro for the official visitation of St. Anne Academy. She announced that all looked promising and that when the charter was a reality, Sister M. Anne Eva would be appointed the first president of the new college. Later, other sisters would be appointed to the faculty.

During the visitation, Mother M. Leopoldine asked Sister M. Rose Isabel if she would serve on the faculty of the new college. She also suggested that she become its treasurer. Sister M. Rose Isabel informed the general superior that she had neither the experience nor the ability to handle funds but felt that she was qualified to teach. Then, Mother M. Leopoldine suggested that, in addition to teaching, Sister M. Rose Isabel could become registrar, in light of her experience and unfailing success in recruiting students for St. Anne Academy. Sister M. Rose Isabel accepted.

It should be noted here that it was possible for the faculty to cumulate duties other than teaching because there was only the freshman class to teach. They assumed, on a part-time basis, administrative or staff positions as time allowed.

On February 26, 1946, Sister M. Anne Eva wrote to the general superior insisting on the appointment of the following officers of administration: president, dean, treasurer, registrar, librarian. Those names needed to appear in the first college catalog to be printed in April, 1946.[14] She suggested student expenses to be included in the catalog.[15]

On March 1, 1946, Sister M. Anne Eva heard from Attorney Duggan

A PROVIDENTIAL ANSWER

I still remember the joy, mingled with relief, that I experienced upon receiving my acceptance letter from Anna Maria College in 1948. As the oldest of six children, I was torn between my most overwhelming desire to obtain a degree and the responsibility I felt toward my younger siblings. Anna Maria's scholarship offer eased that inner turmoil. It seemed to be the proverbial "providential answer" to my dream of pursuing a career in education. Eventually the four Quintal sisters earned baccalaureate degrees from A.M.C., two of them serving as SGA (Student Government Association) presidents. My sister, Sr. Rollande, is approaching her twenty-fifth anniversary as the College's Registrar. She has served as a senior administrator to six presidents.

— *Claire H. Quintal, Ph.D., Class of 1952*

that the legal papers were now before the board of collegiate authority. Their procedure would be to amend the first charter, issued in 1887, adding to it a clause that would include degree-granting powers. Attorney Duggan's confidence was high and Father O'Leary and Mr. Wellen concurred with him that prospects were indeed bright! On March 8, the executed Certificate of Change of Purpose was filed in the Office of the Commissioner of Corporations marking a giant step forward.

All the while, Sister M. Anne Eva was thinking in terms of a curriculum, programs, and courses for the new college. The following letter to Father O'Leary dated March 7, 1946, outlined her efforts: [16]

While waiting for action to be taken on our proposed college charter by the board of collegiate authority, I intend to begin preparing a tentative program of courses. It is my opinion that it might be wise to adhere to a strictly classical culture until it is possible to erect a building containing laboratories and equipment essential to a specialized course in the sciences. *

Thus, for the first two years, we would offer courses leading to the degrees of Bachelor of Arts and Bachelor of Music only. The program of courses would be rigidly classical and would consist of general basic courses in the first year, offering programs of concentration in English, foreign languages, mathematics, religious education, and philosophy for the other years.

The catalog for the year 1946-47 if, please God, the college opens in September, will contain a brief outline of the general courses and a few electives, as only freshmen will be accepted, and they will choose their respective fields of concentration at the end of the first year.

Would you please let me know if I am thinking along the right lines. If not, may I ask you to kindly continue to assist my inexperience with your guidance as I would not like to make any serious blunders that would have unpleasant consequences in the future....

* It should be noted, however, that at the first graduation on May 30, 1950, three students received degrees in the sciences—one in biology (Rose Marie Tanner) and two in chemistry (Theresa Perrault and Jane Trotta). With the arrival of Sister M. Claire on campus, the intermittent semester stays of Sister Irene Marie (Socquet) and Sister M. Rose Bernadette (Madore), and the acquisition of equipment and materials for the temporary laboratory building (known as Pasteur Hall), it had been possible to satisfy the requirements of the degree in science.

Always bearing in mind the importance of the proposed charter, Sister M. Anne Eva followed its progress through the legal stages. She kept in touch with the general superior to whom she wrote on March 29, 1946, that, at its meeting of March 28, the board of collegiate authority questioned the broadness of her demands regarding the charter—she was asking for authorization to confer such degrees as were usually conferred by colleges in the Commonwealth of Massachusetts.

In a letter dated April 3, 1946, Father O'Leary told Sister M. Anne Eva that Attorney Duggan thought it necessary to have a meeting to prepare for the the board's investigator, Patrick Sullivan, and also for the board of collegiate authority. Father O'Leary said that:

...some members might wish to restrict the degrees granted by the college to bachelor's degrees. Personally, I would not favor such a limitation even though I know you would

not attempt to offer graduate work towards a master's degree for many years, if at all.

As late as April 12, 1946, Sister M. Anne Eva told the general superior that the members of the board of collegiate authority were unanimous in their belief that the petition was too broad in scope. They preferred not to grant such extensive powers. Attorney Duggan recommended prudence and Father O'Leary wondered what Sister M. Anne Eva would decide. She was firm in her decision to maintain the petition as originally stated. Father O'Leary was delighted with her decision. However, he told her that she might have to face some embarrassment, if she were turned down and that she might even risk further delays.

Meanwhile, the board of collegiate authority dispatched Patrick Sullivan, accompanied by Father O'Leary, to seek information on finances, faculty qualifications, curricula, requirements for degrees, and similar matters from Sister M. Anne Eva. The latter was very well prepared for the investigation. Throughout the visit, however, she sensed that Mr. Sullivan was sitting on "both sides of the fence." He certainly would not intervene in her favor and help dissolve the opposition of the board of collegiate authority against

broad degree-granting powers! Father O'Leary himself was so upset that he left at the end of Patrick Sullivan's inspection visit and went directly to see Archbishop Cushing!

The hearing with the board of collegiate authority was scheduled for April 23, 1946. That hearing was to be announced in two newspapers—*The Marlboro Enterprise* and *The Boston Globe*—for three successive weeks.

Understandably, Sister M. Anne Eva engaged in many discussions with Attorney Duggan and especially with Father O'Leary. Attorney Duggan felt that, if the breadth of the charter requested continued to be questioned, it might be necessary to limit the petition to the granting of bachelor degrees. However, Sister M. Anne Eva was not only persistent; she was also farsighted. In addition, the following letter written by Archbishop Cushing to Attorney Duggan on April 18, 1946,[17] demonstrated the archbishop's strong opposition to any charter other than one with the broadest degree-granting authority:

My attention has been directed to the fact that some question has arisen concerning the scope of the degree-granting authority which should be requested from the board of collegiate authority in behalf of the proposed Anna Maria College for Women.

I desire to point out that the legal aspect of this particular question is one which vitally affects the entire system of Catholic higher education in the archdiocese. From the viewpoint of uniformity in an integrated system it is not only desirable, but essential, that our institutions at the collegiate level operate under similar legal charters. As the Chairman ex-officio of the Advisory Board of the proposed new college, therefore, I request that every effort be made to insure that its corporate articles shall include a provision for broad degree-granting authority comparable to that now enjoyed by similar institutions in the archdiocese.

In my behalf, you may assure the board of collegiate authority that the projected college will be maintained and conducted in complete conformity with the high educational standards now prevailing in this Commonwealth, and you may extend to it my personal guarantee that the religious congregation petitioning for comprehensive authority in this case is an eminently trustworthy repository for the educational privilege which it seeks to obtain.

Sister M. Anne Eva, Father Timothy O'Leary, Attorney Duggan, and Sister M. Jean Cassien, provincial superior of the Sisters of Saint Anne in Marlboro, were gathered in Boston, outside the chambers of the Department of Education. The members of the board of collegiate authority were assembled, in closed session, to review requests for degree-granting powers submitted by several institutions and to deliberate on their soundness and appropriateness. Unwilling to wait a week for the letter announcing the board's decision, Sister M. Anne Eva consulted with a member of the board. The latter, aware that it was not his prerogative to divulge the board's decision, said to Sister M. Anne Eva: "...if after the meeting, I come out of the secretary's chambers singing a happy tune, you will know that it has gone well for Anna Maria College." Said member was heard humming a cheerful melody on his departure from the meeting—a sign to Sister M. Anne Eva that there was a favorable decision regarding the charter. In a solid vote of confidence, the board of collegiate authority gave Anna Maria College the power to grant all degrees commonly awarded by the colleges of the Commonwealth; that is, all degrees except J.D.s and M.D.s. April 23 would always remain a red-letter day for Anna Maria College!

Attorney Duggan, on May 7, 1946, wrote to Sister M. Anne Eva to inform her that he had brought closure to the formalities and legalities required for the establishment of the new college. His letter of May 7, 1946,[18] follows:

I am enclosing for your information, and retention in your files, a letter addressed to

---

SISTER M. CLAIRE

*S*ister Claire was important to me. Her room in Marlboro was beneath mine and when I entered the building we often crossed paths in the kitchenette downstairs. We often spent time chatting and I and many other students felt that she was a surrogate mother to whom we could bring our problems and often did.

— *Frances Tasse Spayne, Class of 1953*

*N*o one ever left Sister Claire's classes without being a better thinker....proud to be able to figure out syllogisms, formulate postulates, and willing to argue with the best, confident that with logic, epistemology, and ethics, we would be victorious. No one ever watched the clock in those philosophy classes. We always had something to talk about so we did not concern ourselves with closure...discussions went on and on.

— *Carol Harding, Class of 1955*

Sister M. Claire in the late 1960s.

THE PIONEERING CLASS

*O*ne time, Archbishop Cushing visited us in Marlboro and we asked him for a swimming pool. He told us that we had to walk before we could run or swim. So, in the first few years as the college grew, we of the first few classes had to be content with the basics. However, we did receive a solid, Catholic liberal arts education that has stood us in good stead all these years. We are at home anywhere and in whatever circumstances the good Lord places us.

An interesting footnote is that I received my MBA degree from Anna Maria in 1982. My bachelor of arts degree was in biology. I keep being drawn back to my Alma Mater.

— *Rose Marie Tanner DeCenzo, Class of 1950*

me by the Chairman of the Board of Collegiate Authority, dated April 29, 1946, which formally advises of approval of the petition relating to the Anna Maria College. I have delayed forwarding this letter to you because I wished to make certain that the Certificate of Change of Purpose had been recorded in the Office of the Commissioner of Corporations and Taxation, and in the Office of the Secretary of State.

Yesterday I was advised by Mr. Long's office that the Certificate had been returned from the Board of Collegiate Authority, and this morning I personally visited the Office of the Secretary of State and examined the Certificate for the new college. It bears the endorsement of approval by the Board of Collegiate Authority, and contains a notation that it was filed in the Office of the Commissioner of Corporations and Taxation as of April 23, 1946. This latter date, therefore, becomes the date of foundation of the new college.

Since all legal formalities have now been complied with there would be no objection to the issuance of your catalog or prospectus, and the public recruitment of students may be undertaken. In any statement concerning the foundation and establishment of the college I suggest that the following phraseology would be suitable:

The Anna Maria College for Women is a collegiate institution, conducted by the Sisters of Saint Anne, which offers opportunities and advantages for the higher education of young women. The College was established pursuant to authority granted in Articles of Incorporation under the laws of the Commonwealth of Massachusetts, and through its charter it is empowered to confer all degrees usually conferred by colleges in the Commonwealth except medical degrees and degrees of bachelor of laws.

I have made arrangements to procure a copy of the new Articles of Incorporation certified by the Secretary of State. This document is now furnished in the form of a photostatic copy, and as soon as it is available to me I will forward it to you for retention in your files.

On the same day, April 23, 1946, Sister M. Anne Eva was appointed President of Anna Maria College. Sister M. Rose Isabel, in her personal notes, concluded that everybody in Marlboro and the environs was aware of the plans and rejoiced! The students in her senior class felt so sure that the college would be a reality that several were already planning to matriculate as freshmen.

Earlier, Dr. Deferrari from the Catholic University of America had advised Sister M. Anne Eva of the coming June 1946 Workshop to be held in Washington at the Catholic University of America. Sister M. Anne Eva and Sister M. Rose Isabel attended those sessions. The purpose of the workshop was to review and update the organization, administration, and curricula of all affiliated colleges. No other topics were more opportune for the two sisters who had everything to learn regarding the new college. Sisters M. Anne Eva and Rose Isabel found the presentations, seminars, and other gatherings most informative and enjoyable. They met many sisters from other Catholic colleges who came from several states of the Union and thereby broadened their network of colleagues.

In July and August 1946, Sister M. Anne Eva began securing housing and buying furniture, not only for bedrooms but also for classrooms. St. Anne Academy owned houses for employees, and after negotiation some were given over to the college for the use of students and faculty. The academy also ceded to the college the use of some large rooms for the library, sleeping quarters, and classrooms.

Other priorities, such as, the need for bylaws, student registrations, extension courses, finances, textbooks, and several other disparate matters clamored for resolution by the president, Sister M. Anne Eva who often found herself at odds with the provincial superior who was attempting to settle many of these matters in her own way. Coordination and communication between provincial superior and president were especially important at this time and the lack of both gave rise to much anxiety on the part of the president. The problem became so acute that, as early as 1947, Sister M. Anne Eva contemplated submitting her resignation. In August 1946, Sister M. Joseph Alfred, from *College Marie-Anne* in Montreal, was assigned to the new college and became treasurer and professor of Latin and chemistry. Sister Raymond Marie was professor of French. Sister M. Rose Isabel served as registrar and professor of religion, English, and history. Lastly, Sister M. Anne Eva continued as president while serving as dean and professor of philosophy.

Anna Maria College, the fledgling institution, opened its doors officially on Sunday, September 16, 1946. For the resident students there were no private or semi-private rooms! Construction on the building reserved for sleeping facilities was unfinished and, for the time being, residents had to share a large, sunny dormitory room containing two rows of beds and bureaus, and, at the farther end, a large awkward-looking rack for clothes. Adjoining were lavatory accommodations. Trunks and other luggage were placed behind the beds. Initially, the entering students were somewhat shocked and astonished at the living accommodations. However, the charter class, even on that first day, became very conscious of their role as pioneers. This large sleeping space would, for a short time, allow them to become acquainted, reduce loneliness, and give them a genuine opportunity to be "founders" of a new college. Later in the afternoon, they visited the living accommodations under construction across the street from St. Anne Academy.

A teaching mission, the translation of Mother Marie Anne's vision, was the keynote of all the activities of the faculty of Anna Maria College in 1946. They sought to educate in the most complete sense of the word. Sisters M. Anne Eva, Rose Isabel, Raymond Marie, and Joseph Alfred, with only a freshman class to teach, taught 60-minute periods, five days a week for each course instead of the traditional schedule of teaching a 3-credit course only three times a week for 50-minute periods. They were all enthusiastic, well-prepared teachers, and the students responded to their love of learning. The mission, which was not only to impart knowledge but also to pursue moral, intellectual, and religious development, was deeply etched in the hearts of these educators. Their identity and presence reinforced in the students the hope of obtaining the best that Catholic education could provide in the late forties.

"John F. Kennedy alighted from his car and walked up the stairs beneath a canopy of swords."

IV

STUDENT PIONEERS IN THE LATE FORTIES

With the surrender of Germany in May 1945, World War II ended in Europe, and in the Far East, Japan capitulated in August 1945. The United States was jubilant. Service men and women returned home, where there was much to do. The war years had interrupted the natural flow of events and disturbed normal cycles. New homes needed to be built, materials and supplies of all kinds had to be manufactured, aging roads and bridges needed to be repaired, and new ones had to be constructed. A renewed pioneering spirit pervaded the land.

In September 1946, when Anna Maria College began its academic life cycle, a similar pioneering mood inspired the twenty-four young women who made up the charter class. They were intelligent, vibrant, and full of zest. They seemed to recognize their privilege and their obligation to chart a course for the generations of students who would follow them. They were starting from scratch, and much needed to be done. At the outset, a student government needed to be formed and house rules established to govern the residence. Committees were also needed. They had to begin to build a reputation for their talented singing group, establish traditions, and create bonds with the neighboring colleges in and outside of Worcester. Their strong belief in their

Jeanne Dustin, Class of 1950, first president of the Student Council.

33

own individual and collective ability to make things happen prompted them to channel their talents and exuberance into forming what they believed would be a permanent college environment. This pioneering group of students owned the college! While the founding president and her colleagues worried about locating an appropriate campus and assembling a well-prepared faculty, the twenty-four members of the charter class went right to work on all that was new and exciting in their collegiate world.

A letter from Sister M. Anne Eva to the general superior, dated April 30, 1947,[19] revealed to what extent the twenty-four pioneering students had progressed during their freshman year, in charting a course for their college experience:

...The Parent-Teachers' meeting was quite a success, the parents being a very select and dignified group who manifested considerable interest at the meeting. After the address of welcome, the program consisted of a series of reports on the students' activities; these reports were prepared and read by the students themselves. I shall give you a summary idea of the type of activities carried on this year:

1. Miss Jeanne Dustin, president of student council, gave a report on student government as it exists in its initial stage. A very favorable impression was created by the fact that Anna Maria College has been able to obtain membership in the following organizations in its first year:

a) the N.F.C.C.S.: the National Federation of Catholic College Students.
b) the N.E.F.C.C.S.: the New England Federation of Catholic College Students.
c) the N.S.O.: the National Student Organization.
(These three organizations are student organizations strictly.)
d) the N.C.E.A.: the National Catholic

Educational Association.
(I applied for this at the 44th Congress in Boston and our college was granted associate membership; we cannot become constituent members until we have turned out our first graduates.)
e) Affiliation with The Catholic University of America.
(d. and e. are academic recognitions of the college which give us much needed prestige.)

Accordingly, as the different student organizations have their meetings, each affiliated college must send its delegates. Thus Anna Maria College has several opportunities of making itself known and of establishing some very valuable contacts for its students. As the delegates of other colleges are usually juniors or seniors, ours, as freshmen, are benefiting from their very first year of the advantages that are restricted only to older students in other colleges.

On April 24, there was a national meeting of the N.F.C.C.S. in Toledo, Ohio. Naturally, we were not to send a delegate; but at the preparatory meeting held at St. Joseph College in Hartford, Connecticut, which our delegates attended, the boys of Holy Cross, Worcester, and of Boston College, and St. Michael's, Winooski, and Assumption College, Worcester, voted that the larger colleges pay the expenses of a delegate from Anna Maria College and one from Annhurst College for two reasons: 1) that two more votes might be cast in Toledo for the New England Region and 2) that Anna Maria College and Annhurst...might not be denied the invaluable experience of assisting at the national congress. Miss Dustin went to Toledo then as the Anna Maria College delegate.

In the same letter, Sister M. Anne Eva described other student presentations. The president of the glee club gave a report of the musical activities of the club and the group executed several choice selections to the great satisfaction of the audience. There were reports of the work of the dramatic club and the activities of the sodality of Our Lady. Marie Lagasse, an art major, ended the program by extending a vote of thanks to the faculty.

Before refreshments were served, Father Timothy O'Leary addressed the entire group on the topic: "What a College Like Anna Maria Can Do for Its Students." It was well received and the assembly, parents, students, and faculty, joined in a general discussion of some of the pertinent issues emphasized in Father O'Leary's talk.

It was an opportunity for the students to stress their desire for more extensive social activities. The parents listened with great attention to the wishes expressed by their daughters and concluded that the faculty members were not only good teachers but also good advisors and moderators. The parents thanked them for their concern and interest in fostering the growing maturity of their daughters and recommended that space be made available for dances on campus.

In a letter again addressed to Mother M. Leopoldine, general superior, on December 7, 1949, Sister M. Anne Eva recited the activities of the International Relations Club (IRC) and the glee club which already enjoyed large memberships and were participating in joint activities with similar clubs in the Worcester area college world. For the IRC, the highlight of 1949 was a lecture by Bishop John J. Wright, auxiliary bishop of Boston. He spoke on "The Pope and Peace" to a packed academy auditorium including faculty, students, friends, and the neighboring IRC college groups as guests. The evening was a resounding success and Bishop Wright had his first "close-up" view of the Anna Maria College community. As the war years receded further and further into the past, the IRC became less active. In early 1952 there was much in the Boston press about John F. Kennedy, then a member of the House of Representatives in Washington. The rumor was that he would run for another office, either federal or state. It occurred to Sister M. Rose Isabel, eager to shore up the IRC, that she might ask Mr. Kennedy to speak to the club. To her surprise and joy, Congressman Kennedy accepted the invitation and his lecture was scheduled for March 23, 1952! On the scheduled evening, all was in readiness. In full regalia, some twenty Knights of Columbus stood at attention along each side of the staircase leading up to the imposing entrance of St. Anne Academy. John F. Kennedy alighted from his car and walked up the stairs beneath a canopy of swords.

Inside the building, the officers of the IRC, students, and faculty greeted the congressman while the knights lined the corridor leading to the auditorium. He filed through their ranks and entered a packed hall. There was not an empty chair, even in the mezzanine. The student who thanked John F. Kennedy ended by saying that he could count on the votes of the audience in the coming elections. There was prolonged applause and a standing ovation. The knights led the way out of the auditorium to a parlor on the entrance floor where refreshments were served. At about 11:00 P.M., Sister M. Rose Isabel had the opportunity to chat with the congressman. He assured her that, within the week, the press would announce the new office for which he would run.

That very evening, Mr. Morrissey, chief attendant to Kennedy, telephoned from the academy to Palm Beach, Florida, and told Joseph Kennedy, John's father, about the reception at Anna Maria College. The next day, by telegram, the college received $1,000 from Joseph Kennedy. A few months later, he gave $10,000 to establish a scholarship fund. Sister M. Rose Isabel noted, in her memoirs, that this lecture and reception were the greatest events in the history of the International Relations Club.

JOHN F. KENNEDY

*H*ow could we ever forget the night John F. Kennedy was the guest speaker for the International Club (IRC)? By some strange twist I had just become president of IRC (probably by default because I was only a freshman) and it was my privilege to introduce the speaker. I found my picture on the front page of the Marlboro Enterprise with the future President of the USA. What a thrill! The photo became a focal point for our family "brag sessions" ever after.

— *Carol Harding, Class of 1955*

*F*rom the outset, the music department lent a public dimension to its activities, and thereby to the college. The entire student body became the chorus—each member seemed gifted with a good voice! There were also two smaller singing groups, the glee club and another small choir, later to be known as the Paxtonettes. The director, Sister M. Madeleine of the Savior (Payer), was not only a rare musician but a gifted teacher who knew how to make music a source of joy, enrichment, and growth. She convinced her students that music was really a "sharing" art. Every time that one played the piano or sang or executed music on any instrument, one was sharing herself. The song was always a new song—the piano piece was always a new rendering—never to be repeated even by the same artist who shared her talent always with a touch of the new! Each student had to share totally—to give fully of what she had. Imbued with this philosophy, even the less gifted students produced outstanding results. Sister M. Madeleine directed her chorus and the two small groups in many concerts which were always favorably reviewed by music critics. They brought acclaim and a positive identity to the young college. The concerts were perhaps the college's best public relations tool in those early days.

Sister M. Madeleine presented eighty-five major concerts until her departure from Anna Maria College in 1968. In addition, there were many other concerts and appearances by the Paxtonettes who brought the joy of music to women's clubs and many other small groups throughout Worcester County. The Paxtonettes were the "light brigade" of the music department—they responded quickly—so quickly, that on one occasion the group left in the college van without taking a head count and discovered upon arrival that the accompanist had been left behind! Pressed into service, the driver of the van, Sister Antoinette Marie (Jeanne Tasse), found herself sight reading and playing pieces totally new to her!

Reviews by The Telegram & Gazette music critics of the day, Raymond Morin and J.F.

Mona Mong, Class of 1956,
recipient of the Kennedy Scholarship.

Sister M. Madeleine of the Savior (Jeannette Payer) directs the Paxtonettes.

Sister M. Madeleine of the Savior (Jeannette Payer) directs a joint concert.

Keyes, were always flattering. The following excerpts, from a review by Mr. Morin, prove the point:

The program given by students of Anna Maria College, in Paxton...gave the clear impression that the college is well supplied with interested and talented students. ...Even more worthy of note was the fine work of Sister M. Madeleine of the Savior who directed the Paxtonettes and college chorus with her usual unobtrusiveness and skill....The ensemble of 40 sang with discipline and vitality....Some of their best part singing was heard in Spross' "Let All My Life Be Music."...Most enthusiastically applauded was soprano Patricia McDonald who encountered the technical difficulties of Ah! fors e lui from La Traviata with aplomb...she projected a definite talent in voice and thought. Best of all, there was real joy in her singing....

MARLBORO DAYS

*M*y college days were spent in Marlboro, but it was clear that this was a temporary arrangement and we all looked forward to the day when the institution would have a permanent home. That home was not part of my personal experience. I graduated just before the college relocated permanently in Paxton.

Learning, however, does not need grand surroundings in order to be successful. The nurturing of talent by committed women has led to some remarkable achievements on the part of graduates of Anna Maria College. We lived then in a more structured, more disciplined world which still offered limited options for women. The mentoring received at A.M.C. allowed us, however, to go beyond what our predecessors had experienced, to expect more from life, but also to live responsibly, prepared to give more than we received.

— *Claire H. Quintal, Ph.D., Class of 1952*

In a letter to Mother M. Leopoldine, general superior, dated May 21, 1948,[20] Sister M. Anne Eva referred to the music department in these terms:

...Sister M. Madeleine of the Savior's music majors gave a recital on March 25. These young ladies displayed a rare ability of execution and a mastery of their art which surprised us all. The audience was most appreciative and was kept spellbound in its admiration of the perfect command the students had over their instruments. Their success brought out the high quality of the courses offered by the music department of Anna Maria....

All this time, faculty members were making Anna Maria College an exemplary place to study and learn. The college was building the reputation of being a no-nonsense institution.

Minutes of faculty meetings dated January 12, 1947, and October 15, 1949,[21] disclose interesting facts:

...at the request of the student body, there will be supervised study from 4:15 to 6:30 P.M. daily from Monday through Thursday, inclusively...." (Such a request would never be made fifty years later!)

The Graduate Record Examinations will be taken in the spring of 1950 by all the members of the senior class....

Taking the Graduate Record Examinations proved a way of enhancing the reputation of Anna Maria College—several departments consistently ranked in the ninetieth percentile nationally!

On May 30, 1950, the members of the charter class graduated after demonstrating unusual leadership, maturity, and organizational skills. These young women, in their freshman year, established a student government structure

Archbishop Cushing with the charter class, 1946.

which, even fifty years later, served as the basis of the actual student government organization. Traditions such as Class Day, Baccalaureate Mass, Ring Ceremony (no longer active), and spiritual retreat days date back to the charter class. An alumnae association, complete with constitutions and bylaws, was ready to engage the energies of these young women immediately after graduation. They had organized it themselves in their junior year!

39

*"The mission to educate was still
intact and gained support
through the maturing effects of pain."*

V

THE STRUGGLE FOR
A FACULTY AND CAMPUS
1946-1951

Settled in transformed war barracks, employee housing, and borrowed space from St. Anne Academy, a fledgling Anna Maria College survived its first years of activity. There were many problems plaguing the founding president Sister M. Anne Eva Mondor. What was most urgent and most anxiety-generating for her was not always easy to identify. Even basic amenities, such as telephones and intercoms, were in short supply. Physical energy, drive, and dedication made up for what was lacking in technical support systems.

Visitors from the accrediting arm of the Catholic University of America pressed her in their report to prepare a faculty with doctoral degrees and a librarian with a master's degree.

The pioneer president's greatest hope was in the small number of younger sisters, already on her roster of faculty, whom she expected to assign to the pursuit of doctoral studies. The correspondence which Sister M. Anne Eva entertained

with the general superior, Mother M. Leopoldine, testified to many of her anxieties. She repeatedly stressed the need for preparing these young sisters to assume direction of the various academic departments and the library.

In a report dated December 1, 1950,[22] T.D. Sullivan, S.S.E., of the committee on Membership of the NCEA (National Catholic Educational Association), on a visit to assist Anna Maria College in preparing for review by the NEASC (New England Association of Schools and Colleges), wrote the following:

I spent most of the visit with the president, Sr. M. Anne Eva, who was most helpful and was fully aware of the problems facing the college. I spoke to the assembled members of the faculty and they also were fully cognizant of the difficulties of the college....I was much impressed by the foresight and capability of the president,

41

St. Anne Academy founded in 1888 by the Sisters of Saint Anne.
The college used the library, the chapel, two classrooms, and dining facilities.

Trinity Hall joined with army barracks to Miriam Hall and Pasteur Hall.
Adjacent to the Academy, college buildings provided living quarters, office space,
rooms for teaching music, eight small classrooms, and laboratory space.

Chapel at St. Anne Academy.

Sister M. Anne Eva, and by the preparation and enthusiasm of the faculty....

Father Sullivan continued his report by speaking of the faculty:

I do not think any criticism can be made of the faculty or their present state of preparation for the college as it now exists. The plan of training the faculty should be continued in those areas in which greater demands will be met on expansion.

Father Sullivan's statement regarding the training of faculty stood in sharp contrast with the report made by Dr. Deferrari, three years earlier, in 1947, when Anna Maria College was seeking re-affiliation with the Catholic University of America. At that time, the report read: "...this (the faculty) is one of the great weaknesses of the proposed college."

In 1949, Dr. Deferrari wrote:

...Great progress has been made in this connection since then (1947.) Members of the faculty have been trained during the past two years and more are being trained.

It was very heartening for Sister M. Anne Eva to witness such dramatic changes in the reports concerning the training of the faculty.

Apart from attempting to fulfill all the duties involved in caring for the personal and academic needs of the twenty-four freshmen enrolled, Sister M. Anne Eva also faced the nagging realization that the new college needed additional and larger quarters—in short, a campus of its own. She keenly realized that Anna Maria College could not remain permanently housed in transformed war barracks, employee housing, and borrowed space from St. Anne Academy. In his report, Father Sullivan had described the physical plant of Anna Maria College as it existed in 1950:

There are two distinct buildings. The first of these is a frame residence to which have been added army barracks. This building contains very well-equipped rooms for two students each; several rooms for teaching music, and some offices. The second building contains rooms devoted to laboratory space and a classroom for the sciences. In each of the two buildings are found a total of 8 small classrooms with capacity for 10 students each.

These two buildings are adjacent to St. Anne Academy which is conducted by the same religious organization, Sisters of Saint Anne, which likewise conducts the college.

The college uses the chapel and library which are situated in the academy buildings. In addition, the college has absolute use of two classrooms in the academy. Each classroom has a capacity for 30 students. It is my opinion that resident facilities and classroom space are adequate for the present student body, which at present is 49 students (45 women and 4 nuns).

The laboratories for chemistry and biology are small but adequate at present. The working spaces in chemistry are adequate for 16 but actually only 10 are used regularly. The working space in biology is adequate for 5....

To find an appropriate setting for the college, Sister M. Anne Eva spent days, weeks, and months visiting estates particularly in the Greater Boston area. Again and again her hopes were raised only to be quickly dashed. Many factors played a part in this roller coaster ride of hopes and disappointments. The general admin-istration in Lachine, from whom the funds were expected to come, was making great efforts to pay for the construction of a state-of-the-art home economics center in St. Jacques (Province of Quebec),[23] which was approved the same year as the opening of Anna Maria College. To further complicate the issue, the members of the original administration who voted to found the college had reached the end of their terms of office and had been replaced by albeit well-intentioned persons who knew very little about the aspirations and needs of Anna Maria College or of the promises that had been made at its founding. Archbishop Cushing had been assured that the general administration would build an appropriate campus for the new college. However, in the struggle for funds, the needs of the home economics center prevailed over those of Anna Maria College. A letter from Sister M. Anne Eva in answer to one from the newly-elected general superior, Mother M. Liliane, proved the point that the concerns of the college were not properly understood by the new general administration. Her letter, dated January 5, 1951,[24] summarized from the original French stated:

...The third paragraph of your letter leads me to believe that you are under the impression that, in 1946, when the college opened, we were ignorant of the require-ments that such a foundation entailed and of the exigencies of accrediting agen-cies in regard to academic and personnel matters and other needs regarding physical plant, etc. To the contrary, all of these obligations were well known to us; they were explained to Mother M. Leopoldine many times....

Archbishop Cushing repeated them very clearly when Mother M. Leopoldine and I sought his permission to found a college in his archdiocese.

All the documents prepared to obtain the charter and to become affiliated with the Catholic University of America are abundant proof that Anna Maria College was not opened blindly or haphazardly. On the contrary, our college is the result of a plan elaborated a long time ago and meditated upon under every aspect....

Even as Sister M. Anne Eva continued to plead for funds from the general administration, the construction of the home economics center in Canada was becoming more and more of a financial burden for the general administration. Archbishop Cushing and the advisory board of the college persisted in urging construction or purchase of a main building for the college on a campus of its own—detached from St. Anne Academy. Attorney Duggan and Father O'Leary repeated to all concerned that it was on the basis of financial stability and the promise of substantial buildings that the charter was amended to allow for the founding of the college. Archbishop Cushing stressed the need for the independence of the college and its living up to stated requirements: the first being a building promised by the general council and the finances needed for both the college and the academy.

At one point, Archbishop Cushing went so far as to provide the down payment on a property which he considered ideal for the future campus. His disappointment and disillusionment were great when the general administration refused to honor this mark of interest and failed to pursue the acquisition of the property, the Comerford Estate in Framingham.[25] Correspondence between Archbishop Cushing, Mother M. Leopoldine, Father O'Leary, and Sister M. Anne Eva gives some idea of the impasse in which all parties were involved in 1950. In a letter of August 10, 1950,[26] Father O'Leary, always a strong supporter of Sister M. Anne Eva with whom he had shared the travails of the foundation of the college, wrote to her in these words:

...I am frankly grieved about the change of mind on the part of the general council in refusing to buy the Comerford Estate after the archbishop did so much to encourage the Sisters of Saint Anne to establish Anna Maria College. My grief is even greater when I think of his excellency's manifestation of good faith in buying the property with the understanding that the Sisters of Saint Anne would buy it from him.

The whole procedure seems to lack good faith. All I can say is that you and reverend mother provincial ought to write to the archbishop expressing your honest regrets. Certainly, before he loses his interest and confidence in the community of the Sisters of Saint Anne, someone in higher authority in the community ought to visit him and be straightforward in trying to mitigate the embarrassment which he must feel....

It was not easy for Sister M. Anne Eva to explain to Archbishop Cushing what she herself had difficulty understanding. So many facts were unknown to her! There were divergent perceptions of what was needed. In the highly hierarchical governance structure existing at that time in the congregation, the chain of command, when broken, could result in disharmony. In these circumstances, Anna Maria College fell out of favor with Archbishop Cushing, who remained perplexed by this series of events.

On April 27, 1950, Archbishop Cushing had approved the transfer of Anna Maria College to another diocese, if the opportunity presented itself. Mother M. Liliane, general superior, confirmed the above-mentioned date in a letter to the Archbishop, dated May 5, 1951,[27] in which she wrote:

...Your Excellency will no doubt recall that in an interview with Sister M. Jean Cassien, provincial superior of Marlboro, and again in a personal letter to the

Bishop John J. Wright, first bishop of Worcester.

of the congregation gave many valid reasons for transferring out of the archdiocese. She invoked the fact that the Framingham region was adequately served by well-established women's colleges, and that Worcester (the new diocese) would greatly favor recruitment because it was in Worcester county that the Sisters of Saint Anne directed their largest number of schools.

On May 11, 1951,[28] she requested incorporation into the Worcester diocese in the following letter addressed to Bishop John J. Wright, D.D., founding ordinary of the newly created diocese of Worcester:

> *For the past year, as the head of the new diocese of Worcester, you have taken every opportunity to prove your solicitude in regard to the Sisters of Saint Anne who, in large numbers, work in your episcopal city....*

> *Because Sister M. Jean Cassien has informed us of your verbal acquiescence to the transfer of Anna Maria College into your diocese, I now place before you the resolution adopted by our general council...to seek authorization to establish, in your diocese, Anna Maria College founded in 1946, in Marlboro, Massachusetts.*

On May 14, 1951,[29] Bishop Wright warmly welcomed the new college into his diocese:

> *I have your letter of May 11 and I hasten to welcome the transfer of Anna Maria College from Marlboro, in the archdiocese of Boston, to a suitable place in the diocese of Worcester. Please consider this letter as at once canonical permission to establish the college in the diocese of Worcester and a pledge of our cordial welcome, fervent prayers, and affectionate blessing.*

> *I shall welcome immediate word concerning the location of the new college and the*

authorities of the college on the 27th of April, 1950, you had signified approval of the transfer of Anna Maria College from the diocese of Boston to another diocese should we desire it.

...Whereas the establishment of Anna Maria College on the Comerford Estate, in Framingham, already considered to that effect, would entail heavy expenses as to cost of property, repairs, and erection of new buildings all which expenses the budget of the community could not really assume ....Therefore, in conformity with the constitutions of our community, it is resolved to solicit...the authorization to effect the aforesaid transfer....

Thus, on May 5, 1951, the general superior

effective date of the transfer. Please ask the sisters not to make any announcement of any kind until the details of the announcement have been seen by my office.

Also, through the intervention of Bishop Wright, the property in Paxton became available and, on May 25, 1951, the papers for the purchase of the present campus were signed and sealed.

Events from 1947 on had placed Sister M. Anne Eva in the midst of difficulties of every kind: lack of cooperation from those who should have been the first to assist her, lack of understanding of the demands of higher education in the United States on the part of those in the leadership of the American province, and lack of communication on many levels. Her prerogatives as president were not recognized and some well-intentioned persons felt empowered to make decisions contradictory to hers regarding the needs of the college—all of which created a state of confusion and disharmony. Eventually, internal and external pressures took their toll on her health and a serious heart condition brought Sister M. Anne Eva to a difficult decision. In May 1951, she resigned her post and requested a return to the mother house. Her resignation acted as a catalyst in uncovering some of the hidden causes of this discord and, as a result, the veil of misunderstanding slowly lifted. Only the annals of heaven will adequately record the full contribution of this courageous woman to the cause of education in the congregation of the Sisters of Saint Anne. Happily, this last sacrifice on her part precipitated a series of felicitous events which culminated for Anna Maria College in the appointment of a new president, the move to a suburban campus, and the perspective of an uncharted future. Both hope and anxiety coexisted at this time in the hearts of some. Would hope prevail? In the mysterious ways of Divine Providence, the events of the past six years had prepared the college for a blossoming springtime. The mission to educate was still intact and gained support through the maturing effects of pain.

"The college must open in Paxton, even if the faculty have to teach under the trees!"

— Bishop Wright

VI

PAXTON: THE EARLY YEARS

*P*axton! The prospect of moving to a new campus in the diocese of Worcester, where the Sisters of Saint Anne had been teaching in parochial schools since 1881[30] and where they were known to a large population, was exciting to the students and to the faculty. In these early years, the faculty were all Sisters of Saint Anne with the exception of two lay colleagues, Mary Plunkett and Margaret Walsh.

On May 25, 1951, the day, Sister Irene Marie (Irene Socquet) was appointed second president of Anna Maria College, she and Sister M. Jean Cassien, provincial superior, signed the contract for the purchase of Mooracres, a 293-acre country estate, in Paxton.[31] A few weeks later, on July 1, 1951, Sister M. Louise Ida was appointed provincial superior succeeding Sister M. Jean Cassien whose term had expired.

Although very different in style and temperament, Sister Irene Socquet and Sister M. Louise Ida had much in common. Both were at ease in

Sister Irene Socquet in the late 1950s.

college and university settings. Both had degrees and licentiates from the University of Montreal; and Sister Irene Socquet, age 43, had a newly acquired doctorate in chemistry from the Catholic University of America. Both had long experience in teaching on the college level. Sister M. Louise Ida, age 52, had served as dean of the English section of *College Marie-Anne* and as professor of philosophy. Sister Irene Socquet was a foundress of *College Marie-Anne* and, until her residency at the Catholic University of America, had been teaching chemistry, physics, and mathematics there. She was also an accomplished botanist.

Both new appointees were committed to the intellectual life, and both were outstanding religious women. They recognized and respected each other's capabilities and accomplishments.

The quality and reputation of these two women were key factors in creating a sympathet-

College Anthem

Written by
Louise Cristina, '60

Anna Maria, haven on hilltop,
Where gleams unfailingly the torch of truth,
And where thy timeless love,
Gen'rous and strong, leads to wisdom our eager youth.
Here we may savor peace, 'mid transient sorrows,
Live fair and sunny days, joyful in thy halls.
Anna Maria, Thy greatness we revere.

God's smile be ever bright in thy rare beauty
O'er drifts of autumn leaves and snowy paths.
God's might be ever thine;
His strength preserve thee serene in the tempest dark.
God keep thy spirit bold, thy faith undaunted,
Thus we thy daughters pray, with a fervor true
That loyal hearts beat proud 'neath white and blue.

Our hearts we pledge to thee, O Alma Mater,
Anna Maria, gracious is thy name.
How great our joy to plight our fealty,
Thy fairness to proclaim!

ic awareness of the needs of Anna Maria College in the general administration in Lachine. They had a common goal—the growth of the college—and each, in her own sphere of responsibility, supported the other in fostering this growth. There was *entente* which did away with the duplication and inconsistency of efforts that had plagued the first president's tenure.

To a group of city-bred women, Mooracres, described by the realtor, as "a gracious country estate," was far from perfect. It was located on a quiet, dead-end paved town road. There were no lights along the half-mile leading to the house. At night the total darkness was reminiscent of a World War II blackout, and the dominant sound was the hooting of owls. The only source of water was a spring where an electric pump, described as never-failing, brought water to the house. Sister Irene Socquet, the newly appointed president, was born and had spent her childhood on a dairy farm in western Massachusetts. Unlike some of her colleagues, she was at ease on Mooracres. Indeed, she was an excellent choice for the task of adapting the former home of show horses to the requirements of a college campus.

Sister M. Louise Ida, provincial superior, 1951-57.

Fortunately for the college and its future she did not say, "What's the use?" the first time she turned into Sunset Lane and saw only rolling fields and, a half-mile down the road, two lonely wooden buildings, one with a silo attached to its north wall, a fieldstone garage, two horse barns, a heated doghouse, and a corn crib. A nature lover, she enjoyed the sweeping views

ANNA MARIA COLLEGE: FROM MARLBORO TO PAXTON

*T*he AMC student walking around the Paxton campus in 1996 would find it hard to imagine the early days of the college when it was located on a corner lot in Marlboro. It sounds like another country and another time, and in many respects it was. When, in 1952, the college moved to Paxton, the student body had swelled to 89. We were sure we'd need all 293 acres for future expansion, yet we weren't so sure about that silo. If we had to give up "Bergie's" (in Marlboro) where we went to buy a coke and complain about Sr. John's assignments, we would at least have Whitney's Spa in Paxton center—and later the Paxton Navy Yard. What did it matter if, on rainy days, we had to use umbrellas to pass from one section of St. Joseph Hall to another—the cafeteria—because the roof had not yet been completed or later if, when a winter storm iced up power lines and toilets couldn't be flushed, a group of us had to go down to the pond, break the ice, and bring back buckets of water for that purpose? Wasn't that what pioneers were supposed to do?

— *Louise N. Soldani, Ph.D., Class of 1953*

across Pine Hill Reservoir and the surrounding countryside to Mt. Wachusett and Mt. Monadnock in New Hampshire. The paths in the woods attracted her and she often spent her "minute" vacations walking under the beeches and the maples along the trails.

Nevertheless, those early days were a call to courage on many levels. On page 30 of her unpublished notes, Sister M. Rose Isabel, a Bostonian and confirmed city-dweller, described her first Sunday at Mooracres in August 1952:[32]

Left to right: Sr. M. Laurence of Jesus (Lorraine Plette) and Sr. M. Rose Lillian.

As I looked around, I was far from being enthusiastic about the opening of another academic year. Opposite the back porch was a huge hole. This excavated space was walled by cement, the foundation of St. Joseph Hall. To the left of the veranda was an extensive swamp and another behind the garage. Trinity Hall was far from being ready for occupancy. As evening closed, the monotonous drone of frogs from both marshes suffocated whatever enthusiasm I still had.

Sister Irene Socquet, true to her scientific training and her organizational and motivational skills, reviewed the situation, established priori-

ties, and could manage several tasks at a time. She held meetings with the architect, the contractor, and the subcontractors for St. Joseph Hall (the science building) and Trinity Hall (where classrooms and sleeping accommodations were located); discussed the drainage of the swamps with the town authorities; and solicited every one's cooperation in preparing the campus for operation. So much needed to be done!

Meanwhile, the four Sisters who remained in Marlboro packed, labeled, and cleaned the houses to be vacated in September. They sent furniture to be temporarily stored either in the garage or on the convent porch, and in every nook and cranny of the residence. In addition, Sister Irene had bought out all the classroom furniture from the Powers Secretarial School in Worcester. There was need of space to house it, and Mr. Francis X. Powers obligingly stored the furniture in his warehouse until it could be conveniently

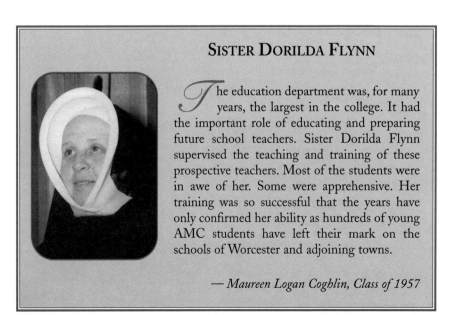

SISTER DORILDA FLYNN

The education department was, for many years, the largest in the college. It had the important role of educating and preparing future school teachers. Sister Dorilda Flynn supervised the teaching and training of these prospective teachers. Most of the students were in awe of her. Some were apprehensive. Her training was so successful that the years have only confirmed her ability as hundreds of young AMC students have left their mark on the schools of Worcester and adjoining towns.

— *Maureen Logan Coghlin, Class of 1957*

The 293-acre country estate, Mooracres, became the new and permanent campus for Anna Maria.

transported to Paxton. Mr. Thomas P. Hurley, contractor for the campus buildings, abandoned the common practice of leaving only one worker on the job and promised to have the existing structures finished into classrooms, offices, and lounges by mid-September. The tiling company followed suit and began covering the floors in earnest. Sister Irene Socquet was everywhere— overseeing construction, reviewing plans, and doing whatever needed to be done to meet the deadline for preparations. She never tired, and her strong physical constitution served her well.

During the last days of August, Sister M. Louise Ida, provincial superior, called for volunteers among the many young sisters missioned in Worcester and Webster, to wash dozens of windows in Trinity Hall and prepare the building for the arrival of students. They responded generously with time, energy, and determination to make Trinity Hall a very attractive facility. Sister M. Louise Ida herself joined the group, thereby cementing bonds of ded-

ication and insuring that the sisters would return for several consecutive years. Several moves were made between Marlboro and Paxton but the last, perhaps the official one, was on September 6. Early on that day, several moving vans turned into Sunset Lane and the sisters, who earlier that morning had closed the doors on their pioneering days in Marlboro, rode behind the caravan. The die was cast—the academic year would open

Trinity Hall with its silo, the fieldstone garage, and the corn crib in the early 1950s.

53

Yearbook staff, 1958.

The greatest hurdle on September 6, 1952, was the science building, officially called St. Joseph Hall. It housed among other important rooms the cafeteria, the kitchen, and the walk-in refrigerator. The roof was non-existent, the staircases were still just ladders, and the front door was blocked by building materials. All the cafeteria furniture had been left in Marlboro for lack of storage space. Sister Irene Socquet consulted with the contractor, Mr. Hurley, who promised to be ready for Sunday, September 28. The furniture that had been left in Marlboro arrived on Saturday, September 27, and, as the workers laid the tile, the movers deposited tables and chairs in their wake. The last worker out of the back door picked up his tools and looked back to see a room on September 29! Bishop Wright's request had been heeded. Earlier, the bishop had said: "The college must open in Paxton, even if the faculty have to teach under the trees!"

First cafeteria, 1952.

Blessing of Miriam Hall on October 9, 1954 by Bishop John J. Wright.

fully furnished on the freshly-tiled floor. Past midnight, when the sisters left the site, there were shades and drapes in the windows and vases of wild flowers on each table. The room was transformed into a very attractive dining area.

On September 29, 1952, when classes began formally, there were 89 students of whom 51 were residents. Seventeen Sisters of Saint Anne resided on campus and assumed the tasks of teaching and maintaining the property.[33] Of the ten faculty members, including the librarian, Sister M. Laurence of Jesus (Lorraine Plette), four already had doctorates and two were at different stages toward the terminal degree. In addition, Sister M. Louis Arthur (Corinne Moll) taught art in Marlboro, for lack of studio space in Paxton. Sister M. Dorilda (Florida Flynn) was at Fordham University finishing the last lap of a

Ph.D. in education. She would shortly find her place on the roster of faculty and become known to hundreds of students whom she prepared to walk into the classrooms of Worcester and elsewhere. Earlier that month, Mother M. Louise Ida had appointed Sister M. Rose Bernadette (Bernadette Madore) to the post of dean of the college to assist the president, Sister Irene Socquet, and to relieve her of the academic day-to-day operation.[34]

In 1952, Paxton did not have a Catholic church. The several Catholic residents celebrated Sunday Mass in a large upper room of Paxton Town Hall with a priest from Christ the King Parish officiating. With the advent of the students on the Paxton campus, Sister Irene Socquet negotiated with Assumption College and obtained the services of a dedicated chaplain,

FIRE!!!

*I*n the early fifties, I served as house mother in the Trinity Hall dormitory. One evening as I walked into the building a strong smell of something burning filled the entrance. I dashed into the room of Sister M. Claire, the dean of students. We raced down through the basement to the boiler room where we found one corner in flames. I ran back to the convent (Socquet House) where the sisters were reciting evening prayer and banged on the door with all my might. Sr. Raymond Marie (Madeleine Carmel) calmly came to the door and softly reproved: "*Mon Dieu, il n'y a pas de feu* (there is no fire.)" "There is—in the boiler room!" I screamed and sped back. Seizing a fire extinguisher, I turned it upside down, but failed to direct the hose toward the flames—guess who got dowsed! Fortunately, by the time the Paxton Fire Department had arrived the sisters, armed with fire extinguishers, had already rushed over and pointed their hoses in the right direction.

— *Sister John (Clarice Chauvin) S.S.A., Ph.D., Professor of English*

Father Thomas Hebert, A.A. He celebrated Mass either in the convent chapel, or in the large room which now abuts the tunnel in the basement of Trinity Hall. Father Tom also taught theology and philosophy, conducted student retreats, and

The queen and her attendants, S.G.A. Cotillion, 1958.

befriended the campus in innumerable ways. On rainy days, when the students were not in class, he played cards with them wherever a table and chairs could be set up.

After the hurricane of June 9, 1953, when the campus of Assumption College was almost completely razed, Father Hebert, for lack of a domicile, lived on campus. During the academic year 1952-1953, the music department conducted courses in a rented facility on Rutland Terrace in Worcester. The students, however, had piano and voice practice on the Paxton campus, wherever there was a spot for a piano and time available. Thus, the sisters' residence housed several pianos and the occupants were serenaded, at strange hours, with music and song. This happened also in the science building where students quietly doing intense microscope work could hear selections by Mozart and Chopin in the background. It was a case of too much, too often! The arrangement was unsatisfactory to both the music department and the rest of the campus and led to serious planning, on the part of the president, Sister Irene Socquet, the faculty, and the members of the board of trustees.

Meanwhile, on campus, faculty members were teaching in Trinity Hall in clean, well fur-

St. Joseph Hall, 1953.

THE GHOST IN MIRIAM HALL

*M*iriam Hall enjoys the singular distinction of having a friendly 'ghost' within its walls! It is a secret shared among the older members of the department and one which they are reluctant to abandon. Miriam Hall favors all kinds of unique sounds, noises, and strange happenings. Doors open gently, the wind plays under high ceilings, and there is always a sense of warm anticipation as one wanders through small practice rooms, classrooms, and a large concert hall. One evening, a faculty member and a piano student were practicing in the building— which is always open for students in need of daily practice. The two heard a beautiful voice in the main corridor and rushed out to see from whence it came. They found no one anywhere. They were alone. Repeatedly, week after week, especially on Wednesdays, they heard the voice. Both teacher and student reflected on the quality of the very pleasing soprano voice and both concluded that it was that of a talented voice major, deceased a few years after her graduation. This alumna loved Miriam Hall and the people who work and study there and they loved her.

Miriam Hall, 1954.

Trinity Hall, 1952.

The student lounge in Trinity Hall, 1953.

A classroom, above, and a dorm room, below, in Trinity Hall.

Sister Irene Socquet and students welcome Archbishop Richard J. Cushing in Trinity Hall, March 7, 1953.

required of Paxton Electric—to the effect that suddenly, around four o'clock, complete darkness fell, not only on campus but throughout the town of Paxton. It was a total blackout.

The town could not generate enough power to light up the campus! There was a scurry for candles and visitors hurried to their cars in the adjoining parking lot. The president realized the need to meet with the selectmen and the board of Paxton Electric. In this Yankee town of Paxton, where sisters were known only from books and perhaps folklore, it was a refreshing sight to see a sister in full habit discussing comfortably with electricians, sanitation engineers, and others, regarding matters with

nished classrooms and also in some of the rooms of the science building. The latter was finally ready for dedication on Sunday, January 4, 1953. Very late, Saturday night, floor polishers were still whirring about, and the final dusting took place after 12:00 A.M. Sunday dawned bright, cold, and crisp. More than 2000 visitors toured St. Joseph Hall (the science building) as well as Trinity Hall which was also being dedicated. Bishop Wright was in attendance to bless the first fruits of so much labor. He congratulated his friend, Sister Irene Socquet, and her colleagues. He also welcomed all the parents, friends, benefactors, and visitors to the campus.[35] Every bulb in both buildings was ablaze—never had so much power been

EARLY DAYS IN PAXTON

*W*hen you came to Anna Maria College in the fall, the first things you saw were the corn fields, tassels tossing in the breeze, just beyond the college sign. Miriam Hall (art and music) on your right. At the end of the road, the farmhouse turned convent. The library-labs-cafeteria building. The plain-vanilla dorm, silo intact, that smelled of new wood and polished linoleum inside. That was the whole of it; that and 293 acres. Anna Maria in the fifties was a place hard to describe to contemporary people. It was sturdy and plain, a simple farm girl among the sophisticated women's colleges steeped in tradition and smothered with ivy.

A decade later, there would be rallies and peace marches up Sunset Lane; but in the fifties, the most activist things we did were to buy Luckies in the smoker and do Elvis imitations. I felt I did the best Elvis imitations because I could curl my lip.

— *Celeste Lydon, Class of 1958*

GRADUATION 1953

*C*ould a student in the nineties imagine graduating from the front portico of Trinity Hall? There we sat under a blazing sun (one day before the notorious tornado of 1953) on chairs with legs mired in the freshly laid black top. Imagine our shock when, as we proudly walked up to receive our degrees, our stiletto heels bogged in the asphalt! What other proof did we need that we were leaving a mark on the college?

— Louise N. Soldani, Ph.D., Class of 1953

First Paxton graduation, June 1953, on fresh black top!

which they dealt on a daily basis. Together they resolved the electric power problems and the blackout of January 4, 1953 was never repeated. A rapport was firmly established between the town authorities and the president, and cordial relations were cemented for years to come. Sister Irene Socquet spoke their professional language and was a quick learner in matters previously unknown to her. However, learning was not only on her side! She was destined to become a legend in the town, on campus, and within the congregation of the Sisters of Saint Anne.

The winter of 1953 was a severe one. Temperatures below zero were frequent and the campus learned that Paxton weather differs from even that of Worcester, only ten miles away. It was usually from 6 to 10 degrees colder in Paxton and the ice storms were legendary. The only source of running water was the "magic" spring from which water was pumped electrically to the buildings. The demand was considerable and on some mornings there was no water! The pump had tripped off. Sister Irene and Sister Bernadette walked several hundred yards down the slope to reset the pump. It required constant vigilance. One day, at 4:50 A.M. when the sisters rose, there was again no water. It was still dark and there was a severe winter storm in progress. Sister Irene and Sister Bernadette dressed to go to the pump but the snow was so deep that walking was impossible and they had to roll down the incline to reach the pump room and the reset button. This pump described by the real estate agent as "never failing," was both precious and deceptive; precious because the campus could not do without it and deceptive because there was no certainty that it would last forever. During a five-year drought in the fifties, Sister Irene Socquet spent many anxious hours determining what steps to take to insure reliability and constancy of supply. To that effect, she had the collecting cistern and the pump house rebuilt and new pumps installed. Her hope was to obtain town water. Several years later, in 1959,[36] at the time of her request to the Paxton water department, the town agreed to accommodate AMC provided the college was willing to pay for installation costs. No water bills were issued by the Paxton water department until this cost had been reimbursed.

THE INFLUENCE OF NATURE ON AN ARTIST

*W*hen I think back on the years 1955-1959 spent at Anna Maria, I realize that one of the greatest influences on my life was nature itself. Music and art students spent much time outdoors just getting to and from class as Miriam Hall was set apart from the little cluster of classroom, dorm, and convent buildings at the other end of the campus. On my daily walks I loved to watch the play of light on Mt. Wachusett and study the changes depending on the time of day, the weather, and the season. It was as if the mountain was speaking to me in its many moods. That daily noting of Mt. Wachusett's mood, I think, awakened the expressive quality of light for me and that has been central to my art-making over the years.

— Mary Dauphinais Attanasio, Class of 1959

Homeowners along Grove Street benefited from the college's request and also obtained a reliable source of water.

Sister Irene turned her attention to the pressing matter of the future of the music and art departments. As stated earlier, art was still being taught in the studios of St. Anne Academy for lack of facilities in Paxton, and the music department taught courses in a rented house in Worcester. Both departments needed to establish a future on campus. After much deliberation and planning with the officers of the college and the board of trustees, Sister Irene Socquet announced that a new arts facility would be built on campus to house both departments. This new building, named Miriam Hall, was completed and dedicated in 1954.

The first graduation on campus took place on June 8, 1953, and was presided over by His Excellency Bishop John J. Wright. The day was beautiful

Myrna Cheung at an art exhibit in Miriam Hall, 1955.

adding a unique luster to the ceremony. For the occasion, Sister M. John of Carmel (Clarice Chauvin) had spent three days applying fresh paint to the wooden extension of the field stone garage which was visible from the graduation area.

During the entire academic year, Sister Irene Socquet and Sister Bernadette Madore studied the requirements for accreditation by the NEASC (New England Association of Schools and Colleges). Anna Maria College was chartered but not accredited. Since this made recruitment difficult, it was imperative for the college to remedy the situation in order to

Variety show, 1959.

insure its growth and reputation. Both President Slavin and Dean Dorr, Dominicans from Providence College, shared valuable information and advice with Sister Irene and Sister Bernadette. Father Slavin was on the advisory board of Anna Maria College and Father Dorr was an experienced dean. Both advised the presi-

dent and the dean of Anna Maria College that their first application would not necessarily lead to accreditation, as was often wont to happen to neophytes. On the positive side, however, the response to an initial application would identify weaknesses and give direction.

Sports Day, 1959.

"You will rejoice with us and help us thank God that Anna Maria College is now fully accredited...."

— Sr. Irene Socquet

VII

ACCREDITATION: THE COMING OF AGE

*T*he most significant event of the mid-fifties was the accreditation of Anna Maria College by the New England Association of Schools and Colleges. Sister Irene Socquet, as president, initiated a first application on March 25, 1953.

On December 10, 1953,[37] she received the following from Dr. Nils Y. Wessell:

The New England Association of Colleges and Secondary Schools through its Committee on Institutions of Higher Education considered very carefully the application of Anna Maria College for membership in the association. I regret to inform you that favorable action was not taken.

On January 14, 1954,[38] Dr. Wessell supplied an explanation:

The committee felt that there are three areas which need improvement and to which the college should give its attention in the immediate future. The first is the library which, although numerically sufficient, is not of the type required of a senior college....The inspection committee reported that the floor space and stack space make it possible to meet this requirement without further expenditure for equipment.

The committee also believed that the catalogue included too many courses that could seldom if ever be given. Many of these descriptions could be removed from the catalogue without decreasing its attractiveness. At the same time the actual situation with respect to the curriculum would be more adequately presented. The suggestion is also made that the catalogue should make clear which instructor heads each field of concen-

Lucy Zee Hsiung '59 (left) and Myrna Cheung Medina '58.

England Association state that there should be at least eight departments in which majors are available, each normally headed by an instructor with a Doctor's degree.

The committee, however, wishes to commend the college for the splendid leadership available to it, both on the campus and off, for its superb geographical location, and for the efficiency and enthusiasm of the members of the administration. We hope sincerely that in time it will be possible to welcome Anna Maria College into membership in the New England Association.

tration and which instructor has responsibility for each course offered.

The committee is also of the opinion that while good teaching is being done at Anna Maria College, more instructors with the Doctor's degree should be made a part of the faculty. The requirements of the New

The president shared the letter with the administration and faculty and together they worked to correct the deficiencies—the library was purged of textbooks and, in the two years following, a much larger appropriation for the purchase of books was made. A professionally-trained, full-time librarian, Sister M. Laurence of Jesus (Lorraine Plette), was in charge. The college catalogue was scrutinized with deletions and

THE FIFTIES

Transportation. Transportation was provided by the college. A bright yellow school bus made daily trips to and from City Hall, in Worcester, running up Pleasant Street and into Paxton. Very few students had cars. The bus favored closeness, social ties, and harmony among the four classes from freshmen to seniors. Every one knew everyone, facilitating a genuine family spirit and mutual support.

The Smoker. The popular student refuge was the "smoker" down in the Trinity Hall basement floor. Card playing, smoking, sometimes studying, and much chit chatting took place there.

Presidential Duties. These duties required multiple talents. Sister Irene and her right hand, Sister Bernadette, could be found at the oddest hours, in the strangest places, using a multitude of keys, a flashlight, and appropriate tools to fix a lock, a door, a wiring problem, a security risk—any and all campus challenges.

— *Maureen Logan Coghlin, Class of 1957*

additions made to comply with Dr. Wessell's recommendations.

On May 14, 1955, Sister Irene Socquet, president, submitted a second formal application for membership of Anna Maria College in the New England Association of Colleges and Secondary Schools. On November 15, 1955, a committee consisting of Newton F. McKeon, librarian and professor of English at Amherst College; Henry C. Borger, Jr., dean of men and associate professor of education at Clark University; and Meribeth E. Cameron, academic dean and professor of history of Mount Holyoke College, visited Anna Maria College at the request of the Committee on Institutions of Higher Education of the New England Association of Colleges and Secondary Schools. Dean Cameron was chairperson of the committee and her report holds interesting comments, some of which are related below. One comment concerns the financial ability to carry out the purposes as set by the college:[39]

Junior Prom 1958
At center: Carol Proietti '60 and Suzanne Chapdelaine Kelly '59.

On this count, the visiting committee, made up of Protestant laymen from liberal arts colleges with all the financial ills that breed is heir to, got a liberal education. We found the financial operations of a college conducted by a religious order both baffling

THE ROSARY, THE SMOKER, AND SOCIAL EVENTS

*W*hen we were graduating from college, the Anna Maria College Guild presented each graduate with a sterling silver rosary. I have carried mine in my purse wherever I went, in the U.S., Europe, Asia, and Africa. It has been over 40 years and so many rosaries! When my son was in college and on his way to noon Mass during Lent, he had a motorcycle accident. His injuries could have been very serious. When I saw him in the trauma center at the hospital, he told me he had lost his crucifix during the mishap. I gave him my rosary which he put around his neck. With the help of Jesus and the Blessed Mother, he was able to heal.

In the early days, some of the best social times took place in the smoker (when we didn't know better), even with non-smoking students. We would sit around the table talking, singing, and playing cards. Among the regulars were Fran Tasse, Brenda McCarthy, Mary Lou Hinds, Annette Trudeau, Ann Cogswell, Ellie Hazzard, and myself. Sometimes Father Tom Hebert would join us for bridge. Brenda McCarthy was very close to her family. Her brothers, James and Father Tom McCarthy, often saved the day for many of us. When we had school dances, Brenda would invite her brother James and some of his friends to escort gals without a partner. We had great times. Although we didn't know Father Tom personally, we felt we knew him somehow. It seemed whenever we were low (allowance-wise), Brenda would get a letter from Father Tom with money in it. She would graciously share the spoils with the group.

— Ann O'Sullivan Giambruno, Class of 1953

Education Club, 1962.

and edifying. Anna Maria College has no endowment in the worldly sense: what appears on its books as the equivalent of income on endowment is a sum for book salaries which the sisters earn by their services but of course do not receive—the

interest on dedicated lives!...Two years ago, Anna Maria College applied for membership in the New England Association, but was judged not ready for admission at that time. Since then the college has been working, sincerely and vigorously, to improve its educational program....We are confident that this improvement has been achieved not merely with the vulgar purpose of satisfying the New England Association. If Anna Maria College is now admitted to the association, the people at the college will not thereupon stop trying. They are genuinely concerned to build a good educational establishment, not just to clear the minimum requirements of an accrediting body. There is real momentum in this institution....

The committee was most favorably impressed by the

DIVINE PROVIDENCE

My story is mainly of the goodness and assistance of some sisters who helped me after I overcame a health disability. They proved to me that I could make it to graduation. I came to Anna Maria College for a summer course after receiving a clean bill of health from the West Boylston sanatorium. A high school friend of mine, Sister Anita Poudrier, had registered for biology and for the sake of friendship I took the same course which I enjoyed immensely. In the fall, I registered as a part-time student and enrolled in comparative anatomy and a few other courses. In November, the registrar, Sister M. Rose Isabel, advised me to matriculate for the next semester as a full-time student. I decided to major in biology and along the way acquired enough credits in mathematics to graduate with a double major. I went on for a doctorate in biology at Clark University and have been teaching biology ever since. As I look back over the years of my life, I detect the imperceptible but real action of Divine Providence through the Sisters of Saint Anne, especially Sister Bernadette Madore, Sister Irene Socquet, and Sister M. Rose Isabel. I am very grateful.

— *Alice T. O'Malley, Ph.D., Class of 1958*

administrative officers of Anna Maria College. They seem to us to be intelligent, candid, zealous for the development and welfare of the college, eager to learn the best practices and procedures of other institutions, and most pleasant to deal with. The administrative officers are all members of the order of the Sisters of Saint Anne. They have been brought up in the spirit of this teaching order; they are sincerely and completely dedicated to the purpose of creating in Anna Maria College a Catholic liberal arts college of high quality. If this leadership continues...the college will be most fortunate.

On December 15, 1955,[40] exactly one month after the visitation of the review committee, Dana M. Cotton, secretary-treasurer of the New England Association of Colleges and Secondary Schools, wrote as follows to the president of Anna Maria College:

At the request of the executive committee and the officers of the New England Association of Colleges and Secondary Schools, it is my pleasure to inform you that at the seventieth annual meeting of the New England Association your institution was elected to membership in the association.

A bill for institutional membership dues in the association will be sent to you in January. The executive committee will always welcome any constructive suggestions you have as to ways in which we may improve the effectiveness of the New England Association.[41]

This membership in the New England Association

opened the door to membership in other prestigious associations, such as the American Council on Education, the Association of American Colleges, the National Commission on Accrediting, etc. In a letter to Sister M. Anne Eva Mondor, first president of Anna Maria College, dated December 17, 1955,[41] Sister Irene Socquet related the good news:

You will rejoice with us and help us thank God that Anna Maria College is now fully accredited....It will now be a mere formality to be accepted in: The American Council on Education, The Association of American Colleges, etc....Our accreditation...crowns the work you began almost ten years ago and which you established on a sound foundation....

Throughout the fifties, the president, the administration, and the faculty worked together to attain status in the academic world and they made things happen. In 1954, evening classes were initiated for part-time students. They met at first on Monday and Tuesday evenings. To emphasize the outstanding work of the best students, an honors convocation was held in October 1955. It became a tradition. The same

Anna Maria College's production of "Backstage," 1962.

John F. Kennedy.

finement in the New York hospital, was published. He sent an autographed copy to his admirer, Sister M. Rose Isabel. She wrote a note of thanks to John F. and he answered: "Do not expect a repeat performance." On May 24, 1956, he sent Sister M. Rose Isabel a large, magnificent sterling silver bowl with a request that no publicity be given for the gift.

At about the same time, Sister Florence Marie Chevalier, chairperson of the sociology department, invited Baroness Maria von Trapp to address her students. The baroness inspected with a critical eye what she visited—especially the artifacts exhibited in the art studio in Miriam Hall. She was not impressed with the collection of Hummels displayed and was quick to express her opinion. However, the quality of her oral presentation inspired the admiration of the students.[42]

In 1956, the campus community celebrated the tenth anniversary of the foundation of Anna Maria College. One of the highlights of the celebration was the concert presented by the Anna

year, the cap and gown ceremony was instituted and the Tau Chapter of *Lambda Iota Tau*, literary society, was officially established.

One memorable visit occurred in the spring of 1955 when Senator John F. Kennedy revisited Anna Maria College. Once again he displayed much interest in the young college, where he was so well received on March 23, 1952, in Marlboro. The senator was greeted enthusiastically by the International Relations Club. A few months earlier he had spent a long period confined in a New York hospital for a back injury suffered during World War II and he was still obviously in pain. However, he addressed the members of the club (the largest on campus). He graciously accepted to have his picture taken with Mona Mong, that year's recipient of the Joseph P. Kennedy, Jr. scholarship. A reception in Miriam Hall crowned the event and the senator extended his visit late into the evening. In the spring of 1956, Senator Kennedy's book, *Profiles in Courage*, written during his months of con-

Baroness Maria Von Trapp, 1955.

Above: Foundress and Cushing Halls
Below: Archbishop Wright blessing Foundress Hall, March 24, 1957.

Maria College chorus in Boston's Jordan Hall, with the Right Reverend Monsignor Timothy F. O'Leary presiding. It was a rare joy for Father O'Leary to witness the growth of the college which he had nurtured in its early years.

In 1957, to mark the opening of Foundress Hall, an all-purpose building, there was a week-long fine arts festival. Foundress Hall housed a large auditorium, an attractive lounge, chaplain's quarters, business and faculty offices, a smoker, and three large classrooms. Beginning in 1957, and for many years thereafter, Mass was celebrated on a regular basis in the auditorium until a chapel was built in Cardinal Cushing Hall in 1963.

All in all, the campus was a busy one—extracurricular activities including dramatics, the glee club, the Paxtonettes, and the departmental clubs, in addition to the sodality, the mission club, and others, kept the students interested and

focused. The Medora A. Feehan Lecture series, funded by Bishop John. J. Wright, attracted some outstanding speakers, including Regine Pernoud from *La Sorbonne* in France and Alice

Graduation, 1961.

Curtayne from Ireland. Students attended these lectures as a body. All of these organizations enhanced the character of Anna Maria College, and many facets of these activities found expression in the college's literary publication: *The Word*, founded in December, 1951. Sister M. John of Carmel (Clarice Chauvin) was not only the moderator of this publication which enjoyed a high reputation as a classical journal, but she also served as its guiding spirit. *The Word* delighted its readers for several decades.

In 1959, Anna Maria College was re-evaluated and re-accredited for a period of ten years. As a result of the pursuit and the attainment of regional accreditation, the college broadened its academic offerings, expanded its involvement in

the broader academic community where it enjoyed an enviable status, developed its physical facilities, and entered the sixties as a healthy institution. It had some problems (there was never enough money!) but the programs were sound and the faculty better and better trained. The college looked forward to a bright and dynamic future.

There was yet no way to foretell that Vatican II, in progress, would soon introduce major changes affecting the Catholic world and also all Catholic institutions. In the years ahead, Anna Maria College would be called upon to redefine and clarify the mission which now directed all its endeavors.

THE VARIETY SHOW —A LONG STANDING TRADITION AT AMC

The precursor of the Variety Shows that were to be the highlight of each year was a minstrel show mounted on the Marlboro campus, in 1951. A popular form of entertainment in the late forties and fifties it provided a showcase for the talented as well as the not-so-talented and, like all variety shows to follow, it was student-scripted, directed, and financed. Indulgent parents and friends of students and the fledgling college provided an enthusiastic audience.

It was not until 1955, however, that the Variety Show began its long tenure as the event of the year. To break up the monotony and dreariness of the often snowbound Paxton campus, but more especially to celebrate in proper manner that most festive of saints' days, March 17, students once again banded together to entertain themselves and the entire college community. So successful was this show that each year thereafter students tried to outdo the previous year's performance.

As individual classes grew in size, the Variety Show took on the nature of a competition among them, with faculty—and later, alumni—as judges. Skits, which were to be no longer than 20 minutes, were evaluated for originality, costuming, staging (sets as well as music and dancing), and participation. Rivalries were strong, and audiences large (as many as 600 on Saturday night) and enthusiastic as they tried to influence the judging by the decibels of their approval.

Preparation for this show could begin no earlier than the start of the January semester. The Student Government Association would select a theme for the year—often in the form of a phrase that was to be completed—and each class would then set about writing a script that would require as many students as possible to mount the production. Music could be based on Broadway shows but lyrics had to be original. Dance routines (and there were many) were developed by students dancers and were often of a class worthy of Radio City. More often than not there was a touch of good-natured satire of faculty and administration woven through the script. One student, usually a senior, was chairperson of the event; it was his or her job to see that all classes had equal stage time for rehearsals, were on schedule to meet the performance deadline and to assure that there would be no duplication of program. In addition, each class had a chairperson who had to "rally the troops," and assure that subcommittees on the various elements of a program were not shirking their duties. Not surprisingly, perhaps, this person was called on to arbiter disputes among budding prima donnas. Though classed as an "extracurricular" activity, the Variety Show was not only a showcase for talent, and an opportunity for building class spirit, but an occasion for participants to practice the creativity, leadership, and interpersonal skills that have characterized so many AMC graduates.

— *Louise N. Soldani, Ph.D., Class of 1953*

Variety Show, 1961.

Left: Second chapel located in all-purpose auditorium in Foundress Hall. Kneelers, a fully equipped sacristy, an altar, and communion rail were available for daily celebration of the Eucharist. Used from 1957-1963.

Places of Worship...

Right: First chapel on campus located in what is now Socquet House, blessed by Bishop John J. Wright on November 9, 1951.

Left: Third and single-purpose chapel built in 1963 in the lower level of Cardinal Cushing Hall. Note the tabernacle in the center of the altar against the wall.

...Through the Years

In 1965, to satisfy the requirements of Vatican II, the marble altar was brought forward, the tabernacle was placed on the left wall, and the statues were removed.

The fourth and present facility built in 1990 on the site of the third chapel was totally renovated to include a central altar, a baptismal font, and new stained glass windows. It was re-dedicated on May 5, 1990.

"Meanwhile, economic, societal, and political events were leading the country, in subtle yet unavoidable ways, to the threshold of extraordinary change."

VIII

PHYSICAL EXPANSION

*A*few years after the transfer of the campus from Marlboro to Paxton, the administration and faculty of Anna Maria College realized that the increasing number of student registrations would soon necessitate physical expansion beyond the few buildings clustered at the end of Sunset Lane.

In less than two decades, between 1952 and 1968, there arose eight new buildings, a central heating plant, and a series of tunnels that served to connect several buildings. The tunnels accommodated water and electrical connections and conduit racks to serve the technological needs of the future. In addition, before town water was brought to the campus, two wells were dug. One, located under Miriam Hall, is 223 feet deep and yields 57, 600 gallons of water per day; the other, in Madonna Hall, is 300 feet deep and yields 115,200 gallons of water per day.

How did this expansion come about? To make it possible there was need for a campus plan, funding, and meeting the exigencies of the Massachusetts Board of Health. Sister Irene

Elizabeth Quinn '67
investigating inside the unfinished Campus Center.

Sister Irene and Paxie in the snow.

BLIZZARDS

The class of 1960 weathered many a blizzard in its four years, usually around St. Patrick's Day. One March, the Anna Maria College campus was covered with at least two feet of snow as two New England blizzards followed one upon the other. Sr. Antoinette Marie (Jeanne Tasse) was up at 5:00 A.M. sitting high on the snowplow. She was rocking back and forth at the entrance to Sunset Lane trying to cut an opening for cars to enter. Meanwhile several sisters were shoveling and making paths from the convent (Socquet House) to Trinity Hall and St. Joseph Hall. The resident students usually left the dorm from a side entrance of Trinity Hall to reach the cafeteria in St. Joseph Hall. The drifts were so high that Sister Irene and Martha Zak, '58 dug a makeshift tunnel on the path between the two entrances. Even if Sunset Lane was open and paths were clear, a parking lot blanketed in snow put a damper on the weekend.

— *Carol Proietti, S.S.A.,*
Class of 1960

Martha Zak '58, Sr. Irene Socquet, and Paxie in their tunnel.

Socquet, second president of Anna Maria College, became the architect of this efflorescence that transformed a budding enterprise into a nearly mature campus. Trinity Hall, occupied in 1952; St. Joseph Hall, in 1953; Miriam Hall, in 1954; and Foundress Hall, in 1957 heralded the blossoming of the next decade. With the assistance of architect Albert J. Roy, Sister Irene Socquet and her administrative team drew up a campus plan which, in those early days, included a stand-alone chapel. All full-time administrators and faculty were Sisters of Saint Anne and their salaries became a partial source of funds for the projected expansion of the college. Trinity Hall, St. Joseph Hall, Miriam Hall, and Foundress Hall were all built with money derived from the congregation of the Sisters of Saint Anne, the salaries of the sisters on campus, and the resources of the college proper. Later, loans were negotiated in partial payment for Madonna Hall and the other buildings which were constructed in the sixties.

Why was there need to meet the exigencies of the Massachusetts Board of Health? What were these requirements? As early as 1952,[43] the Board placed constraints on the number of residential students permitted on campus. Because it was located on the watershed of the Pinehill reservoir, one of the storage reservoirs for the city of Worcester, the campus was municipally constrained to support only a limited number of residents. At that time, the president, Sister Irene Socquet, consulted with Boston's Metcalf and Eddy, sanitation engineers, to resolve the problem of inadequate septic tanks. The engineers advised and drew up plans for the construction of more extensive leaching fields. Thus, in the summer of 1955, a sub-surface filter was installed with chlorination facilities and a lagoon constructed to retain the chlorinated effluent for nine days.

Before the end of the fifties it became clear that a larger residence hall was needed. The rooms in Trinity Hall, built to accommodate

A WALK THROUGH AN UNFINISHED TUNNEL

Elaine Calandruccio and I were walking from Trinity Hall to Cardinal Cushing Hall on one of those infamous Paxton days at the end of winter 1967 when the rest of New England saw hints of spring but it was still winter cold in Paxton.

As we walked along we met Sister Irene and Sister Bernadette. We had a brief discussion on how great it was to anticipate graduation for both of us but the downside was that we would not see the completion of the building project. However, even at this early stage it was possible to walk through the tunnel linking the campus center to the residence. Sister Irene offered to lead us through the subterranean way. She found the entrance, startled a few workers, and pressed forward into the hole. It was easy going for the first thirty yards or so, then the obstacles sprang into place. The biggest problem was that we were not attired for underground exploration. There were piles of sand, gravel, and rubbish and we gingerly went around them. The trek became treacherous as semi-darkness enveloped us. We moved along stealthily and found ourselves jumping over and around mud, concrete, metal staging, and wooden frameworks. We forged ahead into the tunnel darkness and I think that everyone but Sister Irene was beginning to have real doubts as to whether or not we were ever going to see the light of day again.

Sister Irene was having a blast describing the future of this tunnel. We were working hard at moving forward and were on our hands and knees at some points struggling to listen politely to Sister Irene's fascination with the entire building trade. I vividly recall all of us including Sister Bernadette becoming a little giddy as the walk progressed. Amazingly enough no one suggested that we turn around and find the way out. We kept moving ahead and silently made plans on how to greet the search and rescue party that no doubt would be sent after us, if we did not show up for a day or two. When all hope was about lost, we saw a glimmer of light and lo there was the sun! I can hear Sister Irene inviting us to come back after graduation for a completion tour.

— *Betty Clifford, Class of 1967*

two students each, now housed three students and space was at an uncomfortable premium. On July 21, 1958,[44] Sister Irene Socquet brought to the attention of the board of trustees the need to respond to this scarcity of living space on campus.[45] The trustees voted to construct a residence hall, keeping in mind the limits for occupancy set by the Massachusetts Board of Health. The corporation negotiated a federal loan of $450,000 at three percent interest for a maximum period of forty years through the Housing and Home Finance Agency. Bids were opened on October 2, 1958. The proposed residence (Madonna Hall) cost $600,000 and was built by H.U. Bail and Company according to the plans drawn by architect Albert J. Roy, and accepted by the Federal Housing and Home Finance Agency. In 1960, the completed building was blessed by Monsignor Manning, chancellor of the diocese

of Worcester; and already plans were in the making for the construction of a classroom building to be annexed to Foundress Hall!

As early as April 17, 1963, ground was broken for this classroom building (18,000 sq. ft.) which included 18 faculty offices, one study room with 48 individual cubicles, a bookstore, and a chapel for 320 persons. It is interesting to note that provisions were made at that time for television reception and for closed-circuit intramural television. At the same time, a central heating plant was built. The firm of H.J. Madore Construction executed the building plans according to designs made by Albert J. Roy, architect. Earlier, His Eminence Richard Cardinal Cushing had pledged $100,000 toward this building which bears his name. The cost of Cardinal Cushing Hall was estimated to be approximately $250,000. The ordinary income

Sliding behind Socquet House.

Art studio, 1962.

of the college and a short-term loan for twelve months took care of this expenditure. In her report for 1964-1965 to the board of trustees, the president stated that the building was entirely free of debt and she gave the exact cost of the building.[46] It was occupied in the fall of 1963, after the unveiling of a dedicatory panel to honor the cardinal. The college built its own single-purpose chapel in the lower level of Cardinal Cushing Hall and the faculty relished their pri-

OF A FROG

In the summer of 1955, I was enrolled in Biology 102 when a frog dissection was still in vogue. As a student very eager to learn, I was not interested in working with a specimen preserved in formaldehyde and I went along with the teacher, Sister Bernadette, who assured us that anesthetized frogs were the best to view the internal organs in the live condition. Wanting my frog to be the "absolute best" I went in search of one in the campus pond and caught the largest I could see. I numbed it by hitting it between the eyes but it quickly regained consciousness, so I put it in a jar with a wad of ether. Soon I removed it from the jar, rather limp, and placed it on a dissecting pan. I gloated over my catch and full of anticipation, I lifted my scalpel to cut it open. At that moment, it jerked wildly! I was so startled that I jumped off from my stool and screamed frightening the 34 other students in the laboratory. The teacher came over and assured me that it was merely a temporary spasm, not to be repeated. I was almost hanging from the ceiling but—feeling comforted by the teacher—I was soon cutting into my quieted frog and could view its glistening organs, capillaries pink with blood, and heart beating. I was enthralled! Forty years later, the experience is still vivid in my mind.

— *Estelle Airoldi, S.S.A., Class of 1962*

Aerial photo of the new back wings of Madonna Hall in 1968.

vacy within the walls of their new offices. The central heating plant serviced all the buildings on campus, except for the original farmhouse (Socquet House) and Miriam Hall which had their own boilers for heating purposes.

On March 2, 1963, [47] W.H. Taylor, then Director of the Division of Sanitary Engineering in Boston, wrote:

> *...if suitable soils can be found for the sub-surface disposal of sewage, the volume of waste...will be limited only by the area available....In the event the sewage cannot be disposed of by subsurface means, the department will approve the discharge of an additional volume of waste from the college, provided that the effluent from the*

> *sewage treatment plant is further treated by passage through a slow sand water purification plant and chlorinated....If it is found necessary to install a treatment plant, the department will limit the daily flow to 30,000 gallons per day.*

While the college administration and the trustees discussed the best course of action, Sister Irene Socquet had a group of geologists investigate the entire property of 293 acres. Some 40 test holes were dug and percolation tests performed. The results confirmed that Paxton soil actually deserved its bad perking reputation! In 1965, a second sub-surface filter was built and a chlorination building erected. In addition, the plans from Metcalf and Eddy

WHY I LOVED ANNA MARIA COLLEGE

I loved Anna Maria, in the end, for deep-seated reasons: it taught me to admire simplicity and fear the acquisition of things; it taught me to treasure clear thought; it gave me my best friend, Louise Cristina. She was the smartest girl I had ever met. She played the accordion like a fool. She talked about Matthew Arnold and Thomas Merton, and we spent hours deciding what life was really about. She taught me Italian home wine, I taught her beer. Once, her mother sent me a box of chocolates, and while we discussed the fate of humanity, I ate the whole thing. She still talks about it.

— *Celeste Lydon, Class of 1958*

called for slow sand filters between the filter beds and the chlorine contact tunnel. This completed the facilities for the treatment of 30,000 gallons of sewage a day, allowing the college to house 300 residents and a commuter population approximating some 500 students. This ques-

tion of sewage disposal would be one of the more vexatious problems addressed by Sister Irene Socquet throughout her presidential tenure of twenty-four years.

Once again, in less than six years, more residence space was required prompting Anna Maria to lay out the most elaborate construction plans in its history. These called for two wings to Madonna Hall, of three floors each, to house 192 additional residents, bringing total resident enrollment to a full capacity of 300 students. A campus center would be located between Madonna and Trinity Halls. The additions to Madonna Hall would provide double rooms identical with those of the two original wings. The campus center (60,000 square feet) would consist of two diamond-shaped sections with the point of the smaller diamond disappearing into the larger one, and would house dining facilities, a mail room, bookstore, lounge areas, and a coffee shop. Entrances on the level of Sunset Lane would lead to a foyer, where a spiral staircase would connect to the lower floor. From the foyer, one could step down into a fan-shaped dining facility for 400. Plans called for tunnels to link

Bernard J. Flanagan Campus Center, 1968.

83

Alumnae-Student Sports Day, October 1967.

in 1966. In the summer of 1968, a small prefabricated residence built on the hill southwest of Foundress Hall completed these construction plans. The number of resident students was within the parameters set by the Massachusetts Board of Health and it could not be elevated without strict attention to the allowed treatment of 30,000 gallons of sewage a day. The new buildings were named to honor past and present benefactors of the college: Mondor, O'Leary, Eagen, and Duggan Halls, while the campus center honored Bernard J. Flanagan, bishop of Worcester, benefactor, and close friend. The completion of this building program practically

these buildings with Trinity Hall, Madonna Hall, Foundress Hall, and the enlarged central heating plant. These tunnels served not only to house utilities and cables to implement emerging technologies, but some pedestrian tunnels also provided a dry passageway for students on stormy days. The daily exercise of walking gingerly amid all the rubble on campus, coupled with the routine inspection of "what's new, today," kept spirits vibrant and morale high during those two years of construction!

The total cost of 2.2 million dollars was funded through a loan from the Housing and Home Finance Agency, resources of the college, and of the congregation of the Sisters of Saint Anne. The cornerstone for the campus center was laid

Commencement, 1967.

84

Class of 1955 reunion.

doubled the assets of the institution and brought the facilities of the college to a very adequate level of efficiency and attractiveness.

In the seventies, expansion beyond Paxton would be one response to this ever-nagging issue of population limitation on campus. There was no doubt in the minds of the administrators of the time that Anna Maria College would never become a largely residential campus.

Meanwhile, economic, societal, and political events were leading the country, in subtle yet unavoidable ways, to the threshold of extraordinary change. These changes would have a strong impact on all campuses across the land, including that of Anna Maria College.

"*The decade of the seventies demonstrates concretely the efforts made by Anna Maria College to widen its horizons and reach out to many populations not imagined in the original mission.*"

IX

CAMPUS LIFE IN THE 60s AND EARLY 70s

*S*everal events marked the sixties as the most tumultuous period of the U.S. since World War II. A young and dynamic President led the country and created the Peace Corps; Vatican II Council came to a close; the Civil Rights Movement rocked the country; drug use increased markedly; sexual mores underwent radical changes; the Vietnam War tore at the fabric of patriotism; television advanced in use and purpose; and a New Left with strong countercultural principles became vocal. All these events conspired to destroy apathy and create a kaleidoscope of moods on American campuses. Unlike the "silent" generation of the 1950s, the new generation of students, larger than ever and bursting with energy, confidence, and ambition, proved to be very articulate and proactive. A wish to bring "the good life" to all Americans motivated many young people to march through Alabama, Mississippi, and Georgia on behalf of civil rights, and to organize the voter registration drives among Blacks. The demands of the civil rights movement fell on listening and willing ears. Douglas T. Miller claimed that it was civil rights that did most in transforming the "silent generation" of the Eisenhower era into the politically active youth of the sixties.[48]

This was indeed an era of high aspirations. In his inaugural address, President John F. Kennedy urged his fellow Americans to ask not what their country could do for them but to ask what they could do for their country. To Congress he added "these are extraordinary times and we face an extraordinary challenge...." These words confirmed the idealism of the young, twenty million of whom were in their teens at the onset of the sixties. Kennedy established the Peace Corps, giving permanent status to a program which would send young American volunteers to other nations where they would serve as educators, health workers, and technicians. He also gave status to VISTA, the domestic counterpart of the Peace Corps.

As moral commitment came back into vogue on the nation's college campuses, the early sixties, according to Miller, became a period of optimistic protest and moral witness. In the midsixties, Vatican Council II came to a close. It generated considerable controversy among some Catholics with an unexamined faith, appalled and perhaps bitter at what appeared to them to be betrayal. But the vast majority of Catholics saw the council as a new epiphany, which responded to the deeper needs of contemporary Christianity. The council, by its aggiornamento, helped in the adaptation of people to new conditions of life brought on by innovations, such as television with its flood of fast-breaking news and entertainment. The young adult generation of the sixties was the first to be subjected from infancy to television

and to its advertisers both of which largely promoted hedonistic gratification. Again, Miller points out that in the last half of the decade, sexual gratification and drug-taking became part of a new libertarian doctrine.[49] Public nudity and the use of four-letter words were intended to challenge the older generation. America was polarized and caught in a giant whirlpool of anger and change. There existed a nation within a nation; a counterculture created an alternative lifestyle and challenged some of the most cherished values of the dominant culture. Traditional verities were no longer sacred. Patriotism came under assault; young men publicly burnt their draft cards; soldiers deserted the armed forces; young people wore American flags on the seats of their jeans. Despite strong parental opposition, children dressed as they wanted, grew their hair long, smoked marijuana, and abandoned college to become radical political activists or to live as hippies. This tumultuous minority movement would have a profound and lasting effect on the values and the very structure of American society. Marshall Smelser and Joan Gunderson,[50] state that resistance to the war in Vietnam pervaded life in America like a spreading stain. It was the fourth bloodiest war in American history. Idealism faded into turbulence on campuses across the country where there were peace demonstrations, sit-ins, the take-over of buildings, looting, etc. Americans of every faction found a great gap between their dreams and reality. It was the decade of the streets. Incivility and

On the yellow bus, 1971.

abuse became rampant. Within this broad, fast-moving, national context, Anna Maria College pursued life in the sixties, and the tumultuous societal aspects of the decade had a strong parallel in the life of the college.

Confronted by this turbulence, Catholic institutions faced new challenges. Often, time-honored traditions were abandoned. This was not done necessarily to satisfy student demands. Rather, the issues, in the spirit of the times, needed to be reexamined and passed through the crucible of Vatican II's principle of "freedom of conscience." Such standard features of campus life as the annual religious retreat, class attendance, dress standards, curfews, and some dormitory rules and regulations were reviewed and adjustments made. In time there was even a change in the tradition of no class on holy days of obligation. These holy days were no longer recognized as legitimate interruptions to the academic schedule. At Anna Maria College, the principle of "freedom of conscience" had a great impact on students, faculty, and administration

and was taken very seriously when traditions were discussed and reviewed. In addition, Vatican II engendered critical self-examination even in the field of theology. On campus, students demanded an updated presentation of the Christian message. The theology program was revised to make the message more meaningful and real to a generation that rebelled against formalism and rigidity.

In 1966, a summer Seminar on Vatican II enrolled over 200 persons at Anna Maria College. Several laymen and priests presented summaries of eight of the sixteen documents; group discussions followed, and questions were entertained. It was a remarkable success attributed to the Reverend Roger Racine, chairperson of the department of theology and philosophy and to the dean of the college who planned every detail of the Seminar.

Dr. Francis R. Mazzaglia,[51] in his doctoral dissertation entitled: "The Case Study of a Catholic College Which Overcame Adversity: Anna Maria College 1965-1985" stated that:

ST. PATRICK'S DAY AT ANNA MARIA COLLEGE

*I*n the early 60s and throughout the 70s, St. Patrick's Day was a great event on campus. "Miss Irish" contests were held in the large auditorium. There was no need for the contestant to be Irish. The only requirement was to have fun and entertain those in attendance. I recall the year Nancy Kelly, a math major, won the title of "Miss Irish." We had assembled cars on what is now Caparso Field and decorated them with green crepe paper streamers. Mr. Griffin's white Chevy convertible was duly decorated and Nancy sat on the top of the back seat. We had a car parade around the campus with horns blaring and supporters cheering. Classes were not canceled but students watched from the windows as the parade proceeded.

Another year, Annie Mac (Ann-Marie McMorrow), a beloved teacher and later dean, led a faculty pots, pans, and spoons band from the music building around the rotary and to the campus center. Her baton was a small Christmas tree. At the campus center we all sang Irish songs around the tree. What really made the parade was the group of Montessori schoolers marching behind the faculty "band."

— *John F. Kane, Professor of mathematics*

...over time, the mission of Catholic higher education has changed from being primarily concentrated on the education of Catholics to the presentation of higher education in a Catholic context to people of diverse cultures and beliefs.

This statement was certainly true for Anna Maria College. In 1969, in a self-study report, presented to NEASC (The New England Association of Schools and Colleges) for re-accreditation, the author noted that:

Anna Maria's basic goals have remained substantially unchanged throughout the history of the college. However, the expression of these purposes has been altered radically since the founding in 1946....This change...is not merely superficial, but reveals a change in emphasis through new understandings....The word Catholic, suddenly too narrow after Vatican II, has given way to the word Christian, to define now not a method of training but an ideal of commitment...indeed there has been an evolution in emphasis from the development of personal intellectual growth to that of the development of a mature, enlightened personality....

The decade of the seventies will demonstrate concretely the efforts made by Anna Maria College to widen its horizons and reach out to many populations not imagined in the original mission. Initially, it was not only Vatican II that inspired the change, but the strong need for survival. Vatican II provided an ecumenical context to facilitate the change.

Student groups demonstrated generosity and social concern through many of their activities on and off campus. As early as 1956, before the Peace Corps and VISTA appealed to many of them, volunteers among the class of 1956, Shirley Richard, Genevieve Hetu, and Rosemary

Bobka volunteered a year of service without pay at the Copper Valley Missionary Center in Copper Valley, Alaska. The Center was staffed by Sisters of Saint Anne under the leadership of Sister M. George Edmond. Bishop Wright, always aware of what was going on at Anna Maria, donated a station wagon to the Alaskan volunteers.

In the early sixties, the Peace Corps, VISTA, and other missionary groups afforded to the students an opportunity to fulfill a mission very similar to the one animating their Alma Mater and Mother Marie Anne, the foundress of the Sisters of Saint Anne. These students wanted to empower people of the Third World, and their energy, enthusiasm, and know-how helped to transform the lives of hundreds of people. They worked in Africa, Brazil, British Guinea, the

HAVEN OF PEACE

*P*axton—peace town—that's how my high school English teacher introduced us to the location of Anna Maria College. And for most college freshmen, in the early days, the campus was indeed a haven of peace. We enjoyed many leisure walks around campus and even to the reservoir, as well as the family atmosphere created by the sisters.

One incident in particular deepened my sense of belonging. One day, as my classmates and I entered Sr. John's (Clarice Chauvin) English class, she excitedly greeted us with the announcement that one of her plants that flowers only every seven years was in bloom. Then she invited each one of us to view the lovely flower and to compare its scent to a well-known garden flower. What a warm, human touch! Even now, when I see such a plant, I recall the experience of many years ago.

Prior to that time, I could never have imagined the impact and influence the college and the sisters would have on my life. I have become one of them! Anna Maria has continued to be a haven of peace for me through the years.

— Annette Bibeau, S.S.A., Class of 1961

American South, Alaska, India, and other parts of the globe. The overall goal was to enable members of the third world to be self-sufficient in as many ways as possible. Claudette Renaud, '64, was the first graduate of Anna Maria College to join the Peace Corps for work in India, and Sharon Maher, '66, worked in Guyana. Bettina E. Beauchemin, '66, joined the Extension Volunteers and worked in Mississippi; Helen L. Miller, '66, joined the lay apostolate volunteering in the Jesuit missions, in Jamaica; Charleen Dahlin, '63, was with the papal volunteers teaching in Kingston, Jamaica. After paying off their educational loans, several other graduates served and brought the total of volunteers to an impressive number. On May 24, 1963, *The Catholic Free Press* reported that 18 young men and women from the Diocese of Worcester would give a year of service to the Church. The largest single group was one of seven girls, Barbara Leo, Irene Condon, Edith Mooney, Nancy Loftus, Donna Ford, Cindy Lee Smith, Mary Nugent representing ten percent of the graduating class of Anna Maria College. Through the Extension Lay Volunteers program, they served as teachers in the American South or West.

The year 1965 marked the third summer that Anna Maria College was able to offer four-month sabbaticals to some members of the faculty. The dean of students and chairperson of the English department, Sister M. John of Carmel (Clarice Chauvin), requested to spend her first sabbatical summer working to help integrate Miles College, in Birmingham, Alabama, an all-Black institution which had never had white students or faculty. Reverend Donald P. Gonynor, a leader of the civil rights movement in Worcester, and Dr. L.H. Pitts, president of Miles College, facilitated arrangements for this unique venture. Even before definite arrangements were complete, Dr. Pitts was thrilled about the possibilities. Father Gonynor stated:

The choked-up response of a struggling president of a poverty-haunted southern Negro college to the offer of a sister with a doctorate in English who wants to help his college cannot be adequately stated.

Sister John arrived in Birmingham on June 7 and was requested to teach rhetoric to the overflow of some 40 Black applicants for an NDEA Institute. Afternoons she gave to tutoring and sorting books from a mound of boxes donated by Ivy League colleges. Evenings she spent in Black churches where ministers and leaders planned the strategy of the following days. Saturdays she devoted to voter registration accompanied by a Black guide. She lived in a classroom of one of the college buildings. For Sister John, this venture was not only to give some assistance to Miles College in its struggle but also to bring back a new spirit to Anna Maria College. When asked about the possibility of Sister John becoming involved in any public demonstration during her stay in the South, Sister Irene Socquet said: " If Sister John judges that she should be part of a visible witness...then she certainly has the backing of our order and of this administration."

Sister John returned two years later to Miles College to join the faculty of an NDEA (National Defense Educational Act) Institute for advanced study in English. The spirit which Sister John brought back to the campus provided new perspectives especially for her students to whom she taught Black Literature. Their horizons were broadened and they in turn changed the attitudes of many on campus towards the Black experience.

The decade was one of rapid and substantial academic growth for Anna Maria College. An alert constituency was key to keeping faculty and administrators constantly on the cutting edge of thought and practice in higher education. A comparison of the 1960 edition of the catalog with that of 1969 demonstrates the intensity with which academic growth was pursued. Departmental meetings were held monthly and the curriculum committee met weekly.

This latter committee was, without a doubt, the most important in the growth of the college's academic program. The dean of the college, Sister Bernadette Madore, chaired the committee comprising the heads of the various departments. Together they studied the best new programs for the incoming student body, pre-eminently from middle to lower income families. These programs needed to relate to aspirations of a group by whom education, in many cases, was less accepted as an end in itself, than as a means to an end. Thus, the curriculum committee offered career-oriented programs in several fields. Carried out and taught within the liberal arts framework, these programs favored training in mental arts and skills; such as, precision, objectivity, perspective, analysis, and synthesis.

Faculty, especially heads of department, did not hesitate to propose new programs and new approaches; first, to the dean, who always wel-

Freshman orientation dinner, 1971.

comed creative ideas and whose office was the theoretical testing ground; then, to one or two colleagues, and finally, they were presented to all the heads of departments at the weekly curriculum meetings. These meetings encouraged the initial clashes of ideas as well as varied expressions of strength and conviction. As they progressed, members witnessed the demise of superficial propositions and the creation of a forum for discussion to synthesize the best that all participants could offer. There was never a dull moment during these meetings and, in such an atmosphere, the college academic program grew steadily. At least once per semester, all faculty members met with the dean of the college privately. Any suggestions on curriculum revision, course content, improvement of teaching, and student-faculty relations could be brought up at these informal sessions and later reviewed at curriculum committee meetings for serious discussion.

WHAT ANNA MARIA COLLEGE
DID FOR ME

*T*he Anna Maria years armed me first with the academic background that allowed me to pursue my medical school training and my career as a physician, and more important with the ethical and spiritual values to be a healer to my patients. It is my hope that as Anna Maria grows into the twenty-first century, its mission to provide Catholic education to men and women will remain strong.

— *Elise A. Jacques, M.D., Class of 1969*

Special programs not listed in the 1960 catalog appeared in later editions and by 1969 the following additions had been described: they included teacher training for all education programs; such as, education for kindergarten and grades 1-3; education core programs for concentrators in English, French, history, mathematics, modern languages; secondary education, special education, and music education; certificate programs for guidance and psychology and social welfare. Described also were a new Bachelor of Science in medical technology inaugurated on July 31, 1961, through an affiliation with St. Vincent Hospital and later extended to Worcester City Hospital as well as to more than twelve other hospitals in four states; a pre-medical program; courses in computer programming within the department of mathematics; a student exchange program with Marylhurst, Portland Oregon; a bachelor's degree in foreign languages; and a program including a year of study abroad. Apart from courses in French and Spanish, students now could choose courses in German, Russian, and Italian. Under faculty guidance honor students were eligible to undertake independent work in either the Junior or the Senior Year.

Administrative procedures were also updated during the decade. For the first time, in the academic year 1963-1964, the college used the service of UNIVAC, a Boston computer firm, to prepare student schedules, course cards, class lists, report cards, and other meaningful reports. During this period, with the assistance of Eugene Gardiner of the personnel department of the City of Worcester, the college established official personnel policies for non-academic employees for wages, paid vacations, paid holidays, and compassionate leave.

A year-long effort at self-examination yielded a self-study report for NEASC in view of re-accreditation. Such a study raised questions in the minds of the entire personnel and resulted in communal soul-searching. Thus, the benefit extended far beyond the goal of acquainting the

Sr. Irene Socquet in her office, early seventies.

visiting committee with all aspects of the institution. This visiting committee was on campus March 2, 3, and 4, 1969. On December 5, 1969, at the annual meeting of the New England Association of Colleges and Secondary Schools, Anna Maria College was approved for continued accreditation with no restrictions or limitations. As a sign of the times, the student council requested that the report be made immediately available to them, and that a summary be distributed to the campus community. For their evaluation of the progress made over the past ten years, the president of the college presented them with a comparison between 1959 and 1969. The progress was obvious.

From the time of the founding of the college through the decades of physical expansion, funds for institutional advancement came from the congregation of the Sisters of Saint Anne, the salaries of the sisters working on campus, and college resources proper. However generous all these sources proved to be, they were not bottomless pits and serious thought had to be given to active fund-raising such as was and is practiced on campuses, private and public across the land.

In the early sixties, institutional advancement including active fund-raising took on a serious dimension. Under the direction of the Robert M. Devlin Company, the alumnae were organized and a phone-a-thon was sponsored by Archibald R. LeMieux, member of the Anna Maria College board of advisors. He made available the facilities of the Wright Machine Company where he was chairman of the board

RELATIONSHIPS AND MEMORIES

*I*n 1953, I was a student at a local college. I began frequenting AMC and forged bonds which have lasted until today. I met my future wife, Gloria Zarrella, class of 1955—my most important association—and then formed relationships with the Sisters of Saint Anne in whose mission I have participated for 35 years. There were other enduring relationships with lay colleagues and students, especially the hundreds who graduated from the department of social work which I chaired almost from its inception. Gloria and I have been married for more than 40 years and have seen four daughters and one son attend AMC. One daughter is now on the faculty of the Social Work Department.

Paul D. Hand, Associate Professor

I have watched AMC grow from a fledgling institution to a well-respected one with thousands of graduates sharing with others the rich values inculcated in them during their college days. Having been a student in the early fifties, an instructor in the late fifties, a financial aid administrator for more than 16 years, as well as a parent of students at Anna Maria College, I can truly say that AMC is an unbroken thread running through my life.

In their various capacities, the Sisters of Saint Anne molded my life—chiefly, my mentor and major professor, Sister Irene Socquet. Her humility, sense of justice, and love and awe of nature have remained with me to this day. Another memorable time was when we took students on a retreat to Saco, Maine. Sister Pauline Madore, Sister Patricia Fontaine, and I walked along the ocean shore with retreatants picking up sand dollars or just drinking in the beauty of God's world. While the students pondered the meaning of life and their place in the universe, I was again taken by the beautiful people who are Anna Maria—both students and faculty. Indeed, AMC is more than memories!

Paul and Gloria Zarrella Hand stand on the Great Wall of China.

— *Gloria Zarrella Hand, Class of 1955*

Alumni Reunion, 1972. Foreground (from left to right): Richard Berthiaume, Sylvia Gregoire Berthiaume '60, Joan Crimmin Burke, '60, and Michael Burke. Standing: Dr. Paul Dumas, and Jacqueline Seguin Dumas, '59.

of directors. Pledges were received, missing addresses noted, and news items exchanged among the alumnae.

The Student Government Association conducted a fund-raising activity annually. On April 3, 1965, SGA presented, in the Worcester Memorial Auditorium, the National Players, Inc., in a performance of *Hamlet*. The net proceeds exceeded $3,000.

In 1966, a capital funds campaign was initiated with the professional assistance of DDI (Development Direction, Inc.), a New York firm. On June 30, 1969, the alumnae boasted of an impressive total of $122,240 as their contribution. Major gifts came from Cardinal Cushing, Bishop Flanagan, the U.S. Steel Foundation, Inc., H.H. Brown Shoe Company, and the Charlpeg Foundation. The National Science Foundation granted $1600 to be matched by the

college for support of an undergraduate instructional scientific equipment program. To express their interest in the capital funds campaign, the faculty, under the direction and leadership of Richard Connors and Robert Lemieux, staged a show, *Hello Molly*, and won general applause for their ability as actors, their sense of humor, and their outstanding friendliness and cooperation. The presentation was more than a financial success. It cemented bonds between members of the faculty and stimulated the good will of the students, some of whom lined up for two hours before the show for good seats in the auditorium. This continuing institutional development activity opened new avenues of public relations and insured rewards, not only from the financial point of view but also from the standpoint of prestige and influence.

It was in the last half of the decade of the six-

Variety Show, 1977.

ties that Anna Maria College experienced, to some degree, some of the whirlpool of anger and change which was polarizing America. In her 1964-65 report to the board of trustees, Sister Irene Socquet noted that a spirit of unrest and rebellion had marked many campuses and that it would be consoling to record only progress in cooperation and mutual understanding at Anna Maria College. Such was not the case. She wrote that it would be unrealistic not to expect some reaction to the present national trend and not to witness a critical approach to authority on the part of the students and faculty. In another report, she said that the year 1967-1968 was not one of quiet unconcern in the halls of academe. There were everywhere seeds of deep unrest, of changing times, and evolving standards.

Policies regarding the use of liquor, or distribution of narcotics or illegal drugs on college or

college-controlled property were presented to the trustees for approval and implementation. Curfews and dress codes were also reviewed and policies amended or new rules put in place. Sister Irene Socquet, in her report for 1969-1970 to the board of trustees, wrote that the year could be termed one of confrontation at Anna Maria College. Faculty and students learned how necessary it was to communicate with one another and to respect the other's opinion. Those who normally did not express their views determined to speak up in support of their personal convictions, thus consolidating their own position and stabilizing others in their choice of solid moral values.

On October 2, 1969, the administration of the college issued a statement allowing faculty and students to hold classes or not on October 15, and they urged all concerned to devote the

Light and Truth

The Anna Maria College Seal is composed of a shield bearing a torch, symbol of Light, and an open book inscribed with the words *Lux et Veritas* (Light and Truth). There are within the shield two maple leaves, a reminder of the French tradition in which the Sisters of Saint Anne had their origin. The four red discs at the top of the shield are taken from the coat-of-arms of Bishop John J. Wright, the first Bishop of Worcester.

THE WILL TO WIN

Sweet 16

In 1996, the men's basketball team made it to the Sweet 16 of the NCAA Division 3 Championship. The AMCats had a lot of heart but very little height. The four tallest players were 6'3".

Back Row (l-r): Jeff Padula, Steve Daniewicz, Mark Sweeney, Tom Keane, John Patraitis, Mike Dowd, Tim O'Brien, Jon O'Brien, Anthony Carter.

Front Row (l-r): Jon Economo, Student Asst. Joe Brady, Volunteer Asst. Jay Curran, Head Coach Paul Phillips, Asst. Coach David Shea, Asst. Coach Mike Burlas, Jeff Paulhus.

1997 Commonwealth Coast Conference Women's Soccer Champions
ECAC Tournament
Season Record: 17-4 CCC Record: 10-0

Standing (l-r): Head Coach Joseph Brady, Gretchen Wolosz, Cathy O'Rourke, Kelly Athchue, Stacy Cline, Sherri Kelly, Liz Hickey, Manager Jon Johansson, Asst. Coach Matt Reney.
Kneeling (l-r): Manager Jocelyn Verdolino, Stacy Dullea, Sarah O'Brien, Heather Toomey, Kathy Stodulski, Katie Kelly, Andrea Notidis.
Sitting (l-r): Erin Fowler, Lisa Antonetti, Lynn Dungey, Jen Nelson, Lori Evangelista, Heather Notidis.

day to the discussion of the important societal issues facing the nation. In response to the national committee for the Vietnam Moratorium, sixty percent of the students pledged to participate in the programs planned for the day. A faculty panel, presenting the background of the Vietnam War, was well attended. The Eucharist was celebrated for an end to the war.

On April 16, 1970, Dr. Louis Lomax, former TV commentator and author of *The Black Revolt* and *When the Word Is Given*, addressed the students on " Meaning and misuse."

Family Day, June 1974.

His lecture was both challenging and enlightening. The discussion which followed, however, revealed a person with a bias against most of the traditional interpretations of authority, faith, prayer, and God. The lecture led to a request for an all-night teach-in to clarify basic issues.

On April 29 and 30, 1970, from 9:00 P.M. to 5:45 A.M., discussions in the snack bar were attended by well over 200 students, faculty, and administrators. The organizers included one faculty member and some ten students. During this all-night teach-in, topics discussed included the following: unsatisfactory or irrelevant courses, injustice to certain instructors, some decisions of the president, the goals of the college, the principles on which the college was founded, and the incompatibility of those Christian principles with the hiring of non-Christians. The complaints offered nothing new. The issues that influenced U.S. policy in the Far East had a reverberating effect across the nation's cam-

puses and affected Anna Maria campus life more than subtly. When U.S. troops were dispatched to Cambodia in the area occupied by the Viet Cong, unrest on American campuses, including Anna Maria College, reached fever pitch.

On May 4, a rally at Clark University was followed by another, the same evening, in Madonna Hall on the AMC campus. The result was a request for a general meeting of students, faculty, and administrators at noon on Tuesday, May 5, 1970. The upshot of the meeting and deliberations which continued until four o'clock was an overwhelming vote in favor of a "strike" in protest against the involvement of the U.S. in southeast Asia. It seemed clear that the war would not be ended through the initiative of American political leaders unless the pressure of public opinion made it clear that their policies were unpopular. On May 11, 1970, a secret ballot resulted in a majority of students and faculty

'HELLO MOLLY'

*T*he faculty show was conceived as a musical revue in which the faculty poked good natured fun at the college and especially at itself. The "plot" -- very loosely developed -- was the story of the exile of the main character from the real AMC to a mythical college where he would find true happiness. At that time, the popular cultural metaphor for such a place was, of course, Camelot because of the success of the musical by that name. Hence the title song for the Broadway show became the title song of the faculty musical.

In order to be effective, the name of this mythical college -- Molly Coddle U. -- had to meet several criteria. First and foremost, it had to "fit" with the lyrics of the title song, and specifically with the end of the chorus; the five syllables had to correspond with the words "...here in Camelot" in the original song. That was the first and absolutely essential requirement. Second, it needed a "feminine" ring to it (i.e. Molly) to correspond with Anna Maria so that the audience would automatically make the connection. And finally, it had to poke fun at the college. In this sense it was perfect since it raised the very serious issue of "in loco parentis" in a humorous context. Obviously no one took us seriously; this would have been a disaster.

What impresses me today about the show is that at a time when there was no discussion whatsoever about identity and mission, EVERY faculty member participated in the first year show and all but one or two of us did so the following year. How much better it is to live a mission than to talk about it!

-Robert Lemieux, Professor of philosophy and French

in favor of ending the strike. During the days that followed, emotions subsided and students reported for final examinations at one of the two sessions provided. It was noteworthy that the steps taken during 1968-1969 to consolidate the faculty and give them their own leadership proved to be a source of unity and strength in this year of confrontation. To the parents of the students, Sister Irene Socquet wrote that the challenges presented by this generation of students would be met on their terms of authentic-ity, personal concern, and social responsibility only if we, of another generation, gave gener-ously of our trust, our hope, our love, and our experience.

The decade ended on a somber note. Demographers were forecasting low enrollments for the seventies and financial experts throughout the country were predicting the imminent disso-lution of all private liberal arts colleges, especial-ly colleges for women.

"I have thought of you as a model —a no-nonsense, honest, honorable, caring Christian lady."

— Cynthia Taylor

X

ANNA MARIA COLLEGE AT THE CROSSROADS

The mid-seventies witnessed the end of an administrative era. On June 28, 1972,[52] Sister Irene Socquet submitted her resignation to be effective July 1, 1973. Although she listed several reasons for her resignation, the trustees took no action. In June 1974,[53] she submitted another letter of resignation to be effective on July 1, 1975. This time, the trustees acceded to her wish to retire, after a tenure of twenty-four years. Her contributions to Anna Maria College were destined to become legend. Numerous events were scheduled to thank Sister Irene Socquet for her dedicated service as students, alumni, staff, and faculty attempted to outdo one another in their expressions of gratitude. Later, in 1980, the old colonial house built in the eighteenth century, the oldest building on the campus, was named "Socquet House" to honor the second president.

Sister Irene Socquet served as builder, administrator, risk-taker, innovator, and inspiration to her colleagues and students. Bishop Bernard

Sister Irene Socquet, second president of Anna Maria College, during the seventies.

Flanagan, second bishop of Worcester, characterized Sister Irene Socquet as a woman of many talents and of exceptional character, and a dedicated religious, whose life has been an inspiration to hundreds of young women. A former faculty member, Cynthia Taylor, a non-Catholic, wrote to Sister Irene[54] at the time of her retirement in these words: "Over the years that I participated in the Anna Maria community, and since, I have thought of you as a model—a no-nonsense, honest, honorable, caring Christian lady. You have been and will be an example to me and, I am sure, to the students who have been privileged to know you."

Sister Irene's tenure encompassed the pioneer years on the Paxton campus. It was a time when much had to be done. Street lights were obtained on Sunset Lane; town water replaced pumped spring water; generators to provide power in times of blizzards and summer storms were installed; professional maintenance was provided. (In the early days, the sisters themselves cleaned the buildings, shoveled snow in the winter, raked leaves in the fall, and mowed grass around Trinity and Socquet House, in the summer.) Sister Irene was the chief architect and builder of the physical plant. Her scientific background in chemistry, physics, and the natural sciences as well as her strong mathematical academic background and native ability were a tremendous asset during the building process. She became well versed in plumbing, wiring, and carpentry. She identified every power switch, knew which ones to turn on, and could solve almost any electrical or power-related problem. Her physical strength, her keen intellect, ingenuity, and problem-solving abilities all conspired to support the claim that "she could handle a screwdriver, a Greek text, or the administrative reins of a small college with equal dexterity."

On the academic level, Sister Irene needed to see the logical value of every proposed change.

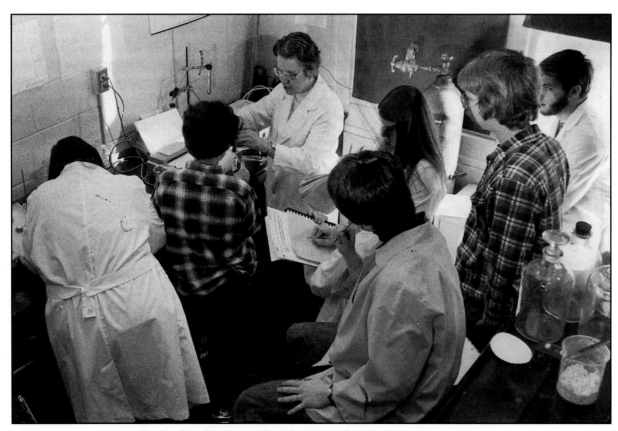

Sr. Pauline Madore with a chemistry class in the mid-seventies.

Variety Show, 1969.

Because of her objectivity, new programs had to be proven desirable and feasible before she would support them. It was only then that she requested approval from the trustees for modifications to existing degrees, curricula, and courses. She enjoyed the trust and confidence of the major superiors in the congregation and of the board of trustees who knew that it was only after much personal thought and collegial discussions that she presented requests to them. She shepherded the college from a single-purpose curriculum to one encompassing not only the classical liberal arts but also serving a vast population in need of professional courses for career changes and advancement, as well as for mobility.

During her entire presidency and several years after her official retirement, Sister Irene taught courses in chemistry and physics. She was also an excellent teacher of Greek which she

Dedication of the Special Education Center, November 1972.

Opening of Spiritwoods, Fall 1973.

academic, and civic. She served within the National Catholic Education Association, the Worcester Consortium for Higher Education, the first ecumenical commission of the Diocese of Worcester, the Association of Independent Colleges and Universities of Massachusetts, and she also served as consultant to religious congregations of women in Worcester.

One might wonder why Sister Irene was willing to work so hard and often to live dangerously, while evaluating risk against possible gains. She was convinced that a Christian college is in a unique position to provide an effective learning environment, to be sensitive to human needs, to develop Christian convictions about contemporary social, political, and moral issues, and to foster in students the ability to articulate and discuss these issues in the market place. Her goal was to see Anna Maria College grow to its full stature as a place where persons, prophetic and convinced, were willing and able to provide students with vision and hope for the future.

taught during her years at *College Marie-Anne*, in Montreal, and sometimes at Anna Maria College when a substitute was needed.

She also led the college during the sixties. Any senior administrator, active through that decade, knows what fortitude and resilience were required to adjust to the deep attitudinal and cultural changes demonstrated by students, and to deal with the generational conflicts which these promoted. It was a time of discontent, disruption, confrontation, and rebellion on the nation's campuses, all of which affected AMC in varying degrees. Buell G. Gallagher,[55] says that, rather than being a primary resource serving the needs of the nation, higher education became part of the national crisis.

While being present to her own constituency, Sister Irene Socquet found time to extend her services to the larger communities—religious,

From December 1975 to June 1988, Sister Irene worked as business manager, a new position created in 1975, and to which she was appointed by the board of trustees. In this position she prepared the way for her professional successors who become vice-presidents and treasurers. As president, for lack of professional help, she had already performed the duties which, as business manager, she now assumed. She prepared budgets, controlled disbursements, prepared projections of income and enrollments; did studies of unit costs and research dealing with financial matters. Among myriad duties, she also supervised the physical plant and its operation and directed all auxiliary enterprises.

She prepared all reports relating to buildings, equipment, and physical facilities (boilers, incinerators, treatment plant, safety, air pollution control, etc.) She had direct responsibility for safety and security on campus.

On June 30, 1988, Sister Irene resigned from the position of business manager and joined the team of operational support, working with the physical plant director. Sister Irene's story, as second president of AMC and architect of the campus, was not restricted to brick and mortar. It is a story written in the hearts of the students and graduates of the college whom she loved dearly and whose joys and sorrows she shared with deep concern. Until August 1995, when Sister Irene Socquet left Anna Maria College, she remained for the campus the witness of longevity, a lasting sign of fidelity, and a source of wisdom, experience, and patience.

On July 1, 1975,[56] Sister Caroline Ann Finn assumed the presidency of Anna Maria College, the first alumna to fill that position. A *magna cum laude* graduate of the class of 1962, she was an English major and furthered her doctoral studies in counseling psychology at the Catholic University of America. She came to the position with a sense of wonder; the campus had undergone many changes since her student days. She moved into a suite in Madonna Hall and remained close to the students, who were very fond of her. She gave much thought to residency for the male students recently accepted as commuters on campus. There was also the question of coeducational housing and parietal rules. Her challenges were those of many Catholic colleges— the chief among which was balancing the budget. The new programs were a source of hope and financial and educational satisfaction for her, for the members of the advisory board, and for the board of trustees, because they boosted enrollment and fulfilled the expectations of adult students.

The seventies offered real challenges to any president of an educational institution engaged in a survival mode. Many Catholic colleges were not up to the demands to insure survival and were forced to close their doors. Events in this struggle acted as in a food chain—none was independent of another and it was important to recognize the linkages in order to take advantage of all of them. A number of faculty and administrators were intimately bound in this quest for survival. Their impatience with the system and a new president often slowed the pace of change and complicated an already difficult role for the president. In her report to the board of trustees for 1975-1976,[57] Sister Caroline stated:

The gradual change which has occurred within the student population, producing an ever-increasing number of part-time students, must affect many of our financial considerations. Although the individual part-time student provides less income for the college, his/her presence requires additional supportive services. It is becoming necessary to balance our desire to increase total enrollment with an acute awareness of the corresponding expenses which this increase will entail.

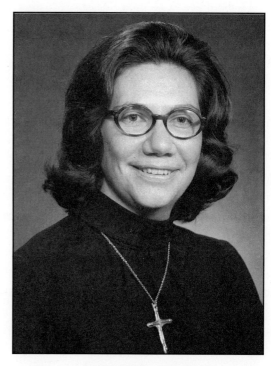

*Sister Caroline Finn,
third president of Anna Maria College.*

*Sr. Bernadette Madore,
fourth president of Anna Maria College.*

The college was in a "catch-22" situation. Since the early seventies, the conviction had grown that full-time education would become the less common pattern, with the possibility of part-time education becoming limitless. It appeared to many that it would be imperative to make part-time education affordable, rather than to abandon it because of the expenses involved. There were varying opinions which split the academic community. Sister Caroline Finn was at an impasse. Since 1973, totals for income and for expenses had exceeded the budget figures because it was impossible to forecast the response to the new courses offered. However, the amounts for income beyond the budget had always, in the past, been greater than the amounts for foreseen expenses. For the first time, in 1975-76 this was not the case. The deficit for educational and general purposes was $281,879 and the deficit for auxiliary enterprises was $56,130. This latter deficit reflected the fact that approximately one

hundred vacancies existed in the residence during the academic year 1975-1976, which was a bad omen.

The year 1976-77 looked bleak. The sponsoring Sisters of Saint Anne, who founded the college and gave it every manner of support had, to date, contributed some $5,000,000 to its advancement. The sponsors foresaw the day when they would no longer be able to contribute the same level of support. It seemed timely for them to evaluate the seriousness of the situation and to consider whether Anna Maria's time to close had come.

In the spring of 1977, Sister Caroline Finn was granted a leave of absence to complete her doctoral studies. One factor in her decision to leave, was the competing visions for the future of the college. The general superior, Sister Colette Dube,[58] appointed Sister Bernadette Madore, who was vice-president and dean of the college, to the post of acting president. Sister Colette Dube told the newly-appointed acting president that the college would no longer receive a loan of 75 percent of the sisters' salaries (over $200,000) nor could it expect any further outlay of large sums as in the past. If the college was unable to support itself, then it should be closed with dignity within a year or two.

The accumulated deficit, in June 1977, was dramatic evidence of a grave situation. The acting president set a goal for 1977-78 which was to create a system to assure a balanced budget, thereby eliminating deficits and the need for loans from the Sisters of Saint Anne. Beginning in September 1977, a computerized information system monitored, on a monthly basis, income and expenses against a monthly budget and a year-to-date budget. Projected expenses were significantly reduced and new revenue streams were identified and tapped. Guidance from two advisors, Joseph Benedict and Shirley Maguire, both of Freedom Federal Savings and Loan Association, and the intelligent efforts of the business manager made this possible. As of July 1, 1978, computerization encompassed payroll expenditures, accounts payable, and general ledger procedures. The system's high degree of itemized detail allowed greater managerial control of revenues and expenditures and provided a basis for long-range planning. For the year 1978-79,[59] a balanced budget was achieved. This was the first time in the history of the college that a budget was approved without reliance on support from the Sisters of Saint Anne. The college embarked on a process of serious financial planning.

The acting president submitted to the college community an action plan for September 1978-1981. It consisted of institutional objectives and goals to be met by 1981. The financial objective was to balance the budget indefinitely, without loans from the congregation. The plan affected academic and student life, including an expansion of campus ministry. It also included development of faculty effectiveness and creativity. A greater self-awareness created a new confidence as Anna Maria College developed a better understanding of its identity, its mission, and its institutional strengths.

For its own purposes, the congregation retained the services of a renowned consultant, David Ruhmkorff, for a study of Anna Maria College. Simultaneously, the college community was launched into the self-study required for re-accreditation by NEASC (New England Association of Schools and Colleges). A sharing of data was possible and one study helped the other. Tentatively, David Ruhmkorff also examined possibilities for merger, alliance, or affiliation as avenues toward survival of the college. In 1978, Sister Caroline Finn resigned from the position of president and Sister Bernadette Madore was appointed fourth president of Anna Maria College.[60]

Two paradigm shifts of utmost importance occurred....In 1973, the college became coeducational, and in 1974, it opened a graduate division.

XI

THE 1970S:
ACADEMIC DIVERSIFICATION
& INCREASED VISIBILITY

According to demographers, attentive to birth rates and differential fertility, the only growth areas in higher education, in the seventies and well into the nineties, were adult and continuing education. The baby-boom of seventy million people born between 1946 and 1964 was followed by a baby-bust in the late sixties, as young people chose small families and zero population growth. Thus, beginning with the seventies, student populations were on the decline. Fewer and fewer baby boomers were left to enroll.[61] The leaders of small colleges, dependent for survival upon enrollment tuition, addressed monumental problems which became survival challenges. Some still healthy colleges closed their doors in anticipation of these challenges; others merged with larger institutions and lost their identity. Others, more fortunate, formed alliances which allowed them to retain their mission and their individuality. Anna Maria College opted to seize opportunities as they presented themselves in the field of adult and continuing education and thus to shape the events of its own future. One major opportunity was the changing demands on the work force by developing technologies. There was need for continuing educational opportunities to favor growth in industry, banking, commerce, and business, where realignment and reengineering were taking place. For administrators caught in the whirlpool of declining enrollments, this need was a motivating survival opportunity. The secret was flexibility and sensitivity to the needs of those who sought the benefit of education. Literally, no one was too young or too old, or too handicapped, or too poor, or too isolated to receive education. Thus, the seventies became a time of extraordinary growth for Anna Maria College.

The college maintained a reputation for academic excellence. To enhance this solidly-based distinction and to meet the changing demands of the national work force, as well as to accommodate the velocity of change now becoming a weightier factor, Anna Maria offered new educational opportunities, more academic alternatives in the selection of occupations, and more options to exercise productive skills in real life situations. It became the goal of the college to make education more relevant and available to a broader spectrum of Americans of all ages and cultural backgrounds. Its ultimate goal was to respond more fully to the specialization interests of its students and the needs of society.

Summer evening classes were scheduled for the first time, in July 1971, to favor the re-entry into the educational world of working adults and professionals in need of formal courses, whether to obtain a degree or to enhance preparation for new careers. The evening schedule extended from Monday to Thursday inclusively to favor longer weekends for both teachers and students. The innovation met with great success.

The use of CLEP (College Level Examination Program) was introduced for the first time. CLEP allowed adults as well as traditional students to demonstrate knowledge acquired in daily work situations, through the news media, from reading, and from life experience. CLEP became the key to a three-year program for applicants who demonstrated ability to

begin college at a challenging level beyond the basic courses.

A three-year degree program leading to a Bachelor of Science in Health Studies for R.N.s was introduced for nurses who wished to obtain a bachelor's degree.[62] The new program was received enthusiastically and the newly-degreed nurses were ready for promotions and prepared for transition to administrative positions. A specialty in anesthesia was also offered to registered nurses seeking a higher level of scientific background and practical experience in the field of anesthesiology. The resources of the department of anesthesia of St. Vincent Hospital were combined with the offerings at the college to make the program possible. It was approved by the American Association of Nurse Anesthetists and the holders of this new certificate were in great demand.

To favor career preparation, the needs created by high mobility, and the velocity of change within the work force, specialties, mini courses, and practicums were introduced in September 1971. A specialty was defined as a series of interrelated courses drawn from various departments allowing students to become acquainted with disciplines very different from their own fields of in-depth study. "Minis" required only fifteen hours of class work to satisfy a limited interest in an area, either to prepare for specialized work, or to update knowledge for new use. Practicums favored on site experience in various fields, enabling inquiry and research, with the goal of greater productivity and qualitative assessment. The 4-1-4 calendar inaugurated in 1971-1972 favored new opportunities for the observation of career areas. The interim session, between the four-month periods, lent

On Campus, 1975.

The choral group in Rome, 1972.

itself to a variety of projects. In January 1972, on a purely voluntary basis, over 40 percent of the student body chose to enroll in one project or another under the guidance of faculty advisors. The first January interim session featured three trips outside the country: Sister M. Colomban (Colombe Theoret), S.S.A. directed a tour to Quebec, Canada, where students lived with French-Canadian families to experience their culture first hand; Malama Robbins led a choral group to study music in Rome, where the chorus performed for Pope Paul VI; Sister Jeanne Tasse, S.S.A., with another group of students, toured Italy to study art ranging from Etruscan to contemporary works.

A number of new disciplines and concentrations emerged:

✦ The department of social relations was established. It provided for specialization in social relations as well as for concentrations in sociology, history, or social work. The Council on Social Work Education accredited the social work major, which became a conduit for acceptance at the second year graduate level of social work in universities. The social work major continues to this day. Many of the graduates of the program have obtained master's degrees in social work and continue to fulfill an indispensable role in the social agencies in Worcester County and beyond.

✦ An interdisciplinary major in liberal studies was made available and allowed students to study in several departments to learn different techniques of analytical thinking. Because of its breadth and flexibility, this major became a means to prepare for more than one career, concomitantly. It continues to be fertile ground for pre-law and other careers, where several disciplines are needed to reach an educational goal.

111

- Psychology, one of the most exciting majors on the college scene in the seventies, was introduced. It was designed to prepare serious students for graduate study. A grant of $4,000 from the Alden Trust was assigned to the creation of an experimental psychology laboratory. The program continues to enjoy an excellent reputation.

- The paralegal program became viable first within the liberal studies department and later, as an independent department, was accredited by the ABA (American Bar Association). It is held in high regard and many of the graduates of the program are today employed in various agencies and as highly recognized assistants in larger law firms.

- The B.M. degree in music therapy, a sophisticated program for students wishing to assist in various settings favoring the handicapped, was incorporated within the music department. It was and is an attractive program which requires four years of study in the music department, in addition to a full semester practicum in an accredited facility working with various physically challenged populations. These accredited facilities are located sparsely throughout the country and, for that reason, several AMC students spend six months in California, Texas, and other areas before becoming certified music therapists.

- The program for medical laboratory technicians (MLT-ASCP), for two-year students and the program leading to a Bachelor of Science in medical technology sciences for four-year students, were outgrowths of the medical technology program established in 1961. They were of interest to students working for an associate's degree and for foreign students for whom the fourth year hospital internship was of less value in their native lands. Both of these programs experienced decline due to the HIV/AIDS-scare, which alarmed laboratory personnel in the eighties.

- The 3-2 program, organized with Worcester Polytechnic Institute, allowed students who met the concurrent academic requirements of AMC and WPI to earn two bachelor degrees in five years; one, in any field offered at AMC and the other, a B.S., in an engineering major at WPI. Three years were spent at AMC and two, at WPI. Prerequisites for admission to the program at WPI were a minimum of four courses in mathematics and five courses in science. The program remains important to a small number of more serious students.

- A bachelor's degree in business was developed in collaboration with the Center for Business Information, Inc., located in Worcester. The students in this program were taught by specialists in the field: business people who brought their work-a-day experience and expertise into the classroom, offering a new link between learning and the real world. The program remains one of the most sought after undergraduate majors.

- A print-communication program, a bilingual education major to prepare students to teach Spanish-American children, and a bachelor's degree in American studies for students looking forward to graduate studies in law, journalism--print and broadcasting--cultural anthropology, advertising, and public relations attracted a number of undergraduate students for several years. In time, these succumbed to reduced market interest due to diminished economic conditions.

These new undergraduate programs were destined to serve new or under-served populations. Besides enlarging the scope of academic life on campus, they also invigorated the college with a new sense of direction and promoted interdepartmental cooperation.

Two paradigm shifts of utmost importance occurred: one, in 1973, and the other, in 1974. Both marked profoundly the destiny of AMC. In 1973,[63] the college became coeducational, and in 1974,[64] it opened a graduate division. Both changes made the college attractive to untapped populations. On May 26, 1973, the board of trustees of the corporation, *The Sisters of St. Ann*, recognizing the economic impact of this important step, voted unanimously to approve coeducation at Anna Maria College after the president, Sister Irene Socquet, had presented the result of an impressive survey conducted with faculty, students, and alumnae. The survey indicated that coeducation was favored by a large majority. The measure became effective in September 1973.

However, it was the opening of the graduate division which significantly increased total enrollments from 1974 to the present. The first Master's degree program in the history of Anna Maria College was introduced in January 1974 to respond to the challenge of requirements which were increased from four to nine courses for state certification of guidance counselors. Education majors seeking certification had two options: to graduate in five years with the added courses or to graduate in four years, without the coveted certification.

On October 2, 1973, after numerous discussions on how to increase requirements without disrupting schedules and time restrictions, the idea of opting for a master's degree in counseling psychology to satisfy the new requirements of the Massachusetts department of education, was presented by Richard Connors at the weekly curriculum committee meeting. It was a precious idea, strong in its anticipated impact. The dean of the college, Sister Bernadette Madore and other strong advocates of the proposed graduate program worked to overcome the fear of the unknown—a major but common hurdle—brought forth by the academic community. The

trustees who were aware of the conundrum and eager for a resolution voted unanimously to approve the concept of graduate education on October 8, 1973.

The approval was like opening a dike! The Master's program in counseling psychology was received with enthusiasm on and off campus. The January 1974 semester enrolled a total of 83 students, 69 of whom were degree candidates. Two other programs leading to a Master's degree were initiated in the fall of 1974: biological studies and business and industrial sciences (later the MBA).[65] Sister Bernadette Madore, who organized the program in biological studies, stated that its main purpose was to make available the new knowledge related to bioengineering and to the ethical and social problems it creates. The future MBA (Business and Industrial Sciences), sponsored by John F. Kane, was intended to meet particular career needs in the areas of finance, management, and marketing. Its objective was to develop functional decision-making and problem-solving abilities in the student. The three M.A. programs, biological studies, business and industrial sciences, and counseling psychology, enrolled 204 students in the 1974 fall semester. Six years later, well over 700 individuals had been awarded graduate degrees from Anna Maria College. In January 1974, with the introduction of graduate programs at Anna Maria College, the campus effected a subtle yet effective transformation from a quiet undergraduate college to a busy center of lifelong learning! Full-time education was slowly but surely becoming the less common pattern, while the possibility of part-time education appeared limitless. Graduate programs instituted since 1974 are still robust and in demand.

On June 1, 1975, Anna Maria College conferred the M.A. degree in counseling psychology upon seven men. This event was significant because these men were the first students to obtain Master's degrees and the first group of men to graduate from Anna Maria College.

Steps were taken to offer graduate courses at the Shrewsbury High School and other off-campus sites. This greatly favored police officers enrolled in the newly created program in criminal justice in response to requests from the probation officers in Worcester County. After consultation with the department of education in Boston and approval of the curriculum, courses were offered on campus and, soon after, at Marian High School in Framingham and at the Belmont McLean Hospital. Courses leading to a master's degree in education were also offered on the Paxton campus. AMC began to develop off-campus sites to broaden its educational base. Beginning with the early seventies and from that time on, college students also developed a broader outlook. In addition, they brought to classes outside burdens; the fact that a good percentage of them were older, part-time students, with family responsibilities made loyalty to the college less immediate. However, what might have appeared to be apathy was simply a manifestation of more diversified interests. In contrast, a positive campus ambiance followed on the heels of the campus unrest and confrontational atmosphere of the sixties.

These times were rich in learning, not only for new populations of students, but also for so many others on campus, including faculty, staff, and administrators. The initiative of admitting men, offering career-oriented programs, and ultimately opening a graduate division brought to the campus new and focused populations—men and women, beyond the traditional collegiate age, seeking job and career preparation. In addition, another factor was of paramount importance, that of enlarging the campus to include a number of sites which, in time, dotted eastern Massachusetts. This factor made it possible for Anna Maria College to transcend the limitations of its location on the watershed of a city reservoir and to be responsive to as many community needs as the college could afford to satisfy.

In the spring of 1972, as part of an on-going effort to keep the alumnae informed, nine alumnae update meetings were held in several locations along the eastern seaboard and in Massachusetts. College representatives communicated with the alumnae by answering their questions regarding the momentum of change on campus. Also in the seventies, the endowment was increased by $80,596 from the estate residue of Archibald Lemieux, Mary A. Neary, and Ernest Socquet. A gift of $35,000 from the DeRance Foundation was applied to the library and allowed the construction of an extension to its existing quarters in Foundress Hall.

In 1977, the first full-time development director, Richard A. Nelson, was appointed by acting president, Sister Bernadette Madore. It was important at this time to share what was happening on campus with the broader community. Mr. Nelson's presence made a difference on and off campus. Through his knowledge of Worcester businesses and other movers and shakers of the city, greater visibility came to Anna Maria College. Richard Nelson opened many avenues for the president, who, in turn, was able to tell the Anna Maria story to a much larger audience. Some influential people subscribed proactively to the goals of the college, and through their financial support, shared in its advancement.

A grant totalling $3,737 from the Medora A. Feehan Fund was earmarked for campus ministry. Another grant of $5,300 from the Fred Harris Daniels Foundation was destined for the department of nursing. Anna Maria College students, through service programs, such as medical technology, education, social work, nursing, and music therapy, were everywhere in the city's hospitals, schools, clinical laboratories, service agencies, and other places where the public is served. The director of development was active not only in fund raising but in all aspects of the college's role and purpose. The eight years that Richard Nelson spent on campus were years of advancement especially in the area of community relations.

The music department through the activities of the AMC Chorus continued to enhance the reputation of the college and to give it visibility.

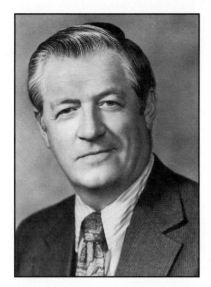

*Richard A. Nelson, first full-time
director of development.*

*Marjorie Guerin, dean of students
in the seventies.*

The Women's Chorus was selected by Governor Francis Sargent to represent the Commonwealth of Massachusetts at the Expo '74 Festival of Entertainment in Spokane, Washington, on August 26, 1974. The same year, under the direction of Malama Robbins, the AMC Chorus joined the Salisbury Singers in a WTAG radio program of Christmas songs and lessons. The program was aired over WSRS, WNEB, and WTAG. Station WSMW (channel 27) in Worcester received the Gabriel Award of the Catholic Association of Broadcasters and Allied Communicators (UNDA-USA) for its program "Christmas at the Worcester Art Museum" which featured the AMC choral group singing with a background of classical paintings particularly suitable to the Christmas season. An album featuring selections sung at the Worcester Art Museum in 1971, and in Rome, Italy, in 1972 was released for sale.

As early as 1977, hours, weeks, and months were spent scrutinizing all college programs, both academic and non-academic to prepare for re-accreditation of the college by NEASC, the New England Association of Schools and Colleges, in 1979. There was much to be done, especially in light of all the new programs introduced in the

decade of the seventies. Just from the viewpoint of demographics and student population, radical changes had occurred. The percentage of traditional college-age persons had already peaked, and the number of adult students was increasing, as the demographers of the late fifties and early sixties had forecasted. Older Americans (from 35 years up) constituted the fastest-growing source of new students in higher education. The main efforts of the decade had been directed toward identifying new student markets, devising academic programs to serve their needs, and broadening the recruitment base. Planning for Anna Maria College, as well as for most small colleges across the land, had meant planning for survival. This included retrenchment in unproductive areas to favor expansion in more promising fields. The resultant self-study report for NEASC was comprehensive in all dimensions.

Already, there had been many discussions about the possibility of incorporating Anna Maria College separately from the congregation of the Sisters of Saint Anne.[66] Those discussions including studies and surveys were generated within the congregation as well as without. A number of other congregations were also investigating the benefits of separate incorporation for their institutions of higher education. For Anna Maria College, this consideration needed to be factored into any future plans. What would be the benefits and the shortcomings of separate incorporation? The mission and the vision which first inspired the foundress of the congregation responsible for the opening of Anna Maria College echoed strongly in the spirit of the college. All the daughters of the foundress, Esther Blondin, including the Sisters of Saint Anne at Anna Maria College who claimed Esther's vision as their own, pursued a mission of Christian education.

In the seventies, Esther's vision continued to inspire their hearts and minds. There was continuity in the mission. It was thirty years since the founding of the college and, despite a crisis in religious vocations, nineteen Sisters of Saint Anne retained appointments at the college to teach, administer, or to serve as staff. To the sisters, placing a stamp of religious identity on the curriculum; on academic, student, and community services; on personnel, athletics, and campus ministry was the basic reason for their presence as religious on a Catholic campus. Each sister was conscious of her identity and the mission of the college. Under the rubrics of separate incorporation how would the Sisters of Saint Anne and their lay colleagues continue to espouse the mission in light of the apostolic role on campus undertaken by the earliest members? How would separate incorporation affect the college in terms of the congregation and vice versa?

It was a very appropriate time for the college to be visited by NEASC. It would allow trustees, administrators, faculty, and staff to see themselves through the eyes of sympathetic, but objective observers and to receive their counsel. There was no doubt in the mind of President Madore that the steps taken in the seventies would reverberate into the eighties. On November 19-21, 1978, there was an on-site evaluation visit of the college by a team of seven persons appointed by the Commission for Accreditation for the New England Association of Schools and colleges. On May 10, 1979,[67] the college received continued accreditation with a strong recommendation to review governance, especially at the level of trustee and faculty participation. The NEASC visiting team had observed that the board of trustees had reserved powers that, from a governance perspective, belonged more appropriately to the president of the college. The main recommendation was:

Glee Club at Channel 27, March 1974.

116

...to define clearly the relationships among the corporation, board, and administration, in order that the institution be given the necessary authority to operate effectively. The present governing structure does not appear to ensure this, and the Commission is genuinely concerned that Anna Maria College assign the highest priority to resolving this central problem. Until such a resolution is achieved, every weakness at the college will be exacerbated and incapable of major amelioration...above all, the governance issue demands immediate attention and resolution.

A weighty agenda awaited the college in the early eighties. President Madore resolved to address the problem of governance on all levels: the corporation, the trustees, the faculty. The chairperson of the board, Sister Lorraine Marie (Doris Gagnon), was very supportive and active in this endeavor.

The period from 1971 to 1980 gave the college experience in seizing opportunities outside the comfortable world of academe. Those years remain in the history of Anna Maria College as a period of challenge and reward—the challenge of discovering new ideas and allowing them to burgeon and mature into fresh and novel ways of presenting knowledge, which in turn became a reward to the college student, both undergraduate and graduate.

"The Commission has asked me to commend Anna Maria College for the significant strengthening of its governance and its much improved financial situation."

— Commission on Institutions of Higher Education

XII

DYNAMIC FORCES: NEW DIMENSIONS

*C*atholic higher education in the seventies felt the sweeping movement of separate incorporation. Jesuits, Dominicans, Franciscans, and many other congregations incorporated their colleges and universities separately from their religious communities. Since 1967, Anna Maria College had taken part in discussions centering on this issue. During Sister Irene Socquet's presidency and Sister Caroline Finn's tenure,[68] research and consultation continued on the subject. Although not new, the concept needed to be explored in all its dimensions allowing both the college and the congregation the possibility of unfettered growth in accordance with their separate but related missions.

There were many advantages to pursuing a separate incorporation for Anna Maria College. The constitution and bylaws which governed the college needed revision and adaptation, chiefly because they were the same as those which regu-

lated the corporation known as *The Sisters of St. Ann.* This corporation was established in 1887 to regulate the affairs of the religious congregation, an entity quite different from Anna Maria College. Since its creation, the college was considered to be merely a function of this corporation. Establishing a separate corporation with bylaws adjusted to contemporary conditions in higher education would benefit both the college and the congregation.

The re-evaluation visit by NEASC, on November 19-21, 1978, mentioned in the previous chapter, precipitated the completion of the project of separate incorporation for Anna Maria College. As a result of this visit, Anna Maria College was granted continued accreditation for a period of three years, during which time the serious problem of governance identified by the visiting team had to be resolved. Excerpts from the report[69] were reminiscent of discussions already occurring on the level of the administra-

THE CHANGING FACE OF ANNA MARIA COLLEGE

*I*f one compared the new AMC trustees to what one would consider "a profile sketch" of college trustees in this country, we were definitely not in the average range. As a whole, we were young, some of us had more experience than others, and we came from a very broad range of backgrounds. But we had one incredible, unifying goal: to transition AMC from a small, liberal arts institution to a mainstream American college while maintaining a value-oriented curriculum and faculty and a mission based in the tradition of the Sisters of Saint Anne.

Within the first few meetings, we were organized into committees and we meshed into a working organic whole with a common objective, to prepare this institution for the new century. And, before we even realized it, we had become more than friends. We had joined the Anna Maria family. There was no stopping our enthusiasm and our commitment.

We had been carefully selected, we later learned, and assigned to various tasks by a strong president and an even stronger chairman of the board. We set to the task at hand with zeal. When I look back on that time, I know we were energized by their leadership.

— Suzanne Chapdelaine Kelly, Class of 1959, trustee 1980–1983

tion of the college and the congregation. They read as follows:

...The present relationship between the corporation, the board of trustees, and the administration is highly unsatisfactory, and, it seemed to the committee, harmful to the best interests of the college....The college does not exist as a separate corporation from the corporation known as The Sisters of St. Ann*....The same constitution and bylaws govern the corporation of* The Sisters of St. Ann *and Anna Maria College.*

...Article IV of the constitution and bylaws of The Sisters of St. Ann *and of Anna Maria College states that the corporation's powers shall be vested in and exercised by a board of trustees which consists, ex officio, of the regular and acting members of the administrative officers of the congregation of the Sisters of Saint Anne in the province of the U.S., the president of Anna Maria College and the chief executive officer of any subsequent institution maintained by the corporation. The corporate powers which are vested in these persons would be exercised at meetings of the board of trustees...there are times when the administrative officers of the congregation of the Sisters of Saint Anne take action on the college when they meet as a corporation to consider business of the congregation.... Should business concerning the college be brought up at the meeting, the business with respect to the college may take place, even in the absence of the president of the college....*

The board of trustees should be the group most dedicated to the college, yet the choice of administrative officers...does not appear to take into account the necessity for concern for the college as a sine qua non of membership on the board of trustees....This means that the philosophy with respect to the college could change every time there is a change of appointments.

...The college, which should be a very strong institution, becomes a fragile one....It is absolutely necessary that the college have institutional independence from The Sisters of Saint Ann*, even while the Sisters of Saint Anne sponsor the institution known as Anna Maria College....The functions, as well as the composition of this board, present problems...the president is not able to choose her own administrative team.*

Sister Lorraine Marie Gagnon, provincial superior, and her council; together with Sister

120

Mariette Mainville, general treasurer of the congregation, joined with President Bernadette Madore to bring the problem of incorporation to a successful resolution. Attorneys for the college and St. Marie Province brought their legal expertise to bear on the issue. Since there was total agreement that the problem needed resolution, the discussions concentrated on the best way to do so. New bylaws formulated by Attorney Charles Burling were in the hands of the committee on incorporation as early as March 2, 1979. They were written to meet the demands of the time, the constructive criticisms of NEASC, and in keeping with the highest standards governing Catholic institutions of higher education. The March 2 draft of the bylaws was modified many times before final adoption. Under the final draft, the president was to appoint all officers of the college without seeking formal confirmation from the board of trustees. On June 28, 1979,[70] official incorporation documents were signed and forwarded to the appropriate department in Boston. In mid-July, upon inquiry by

Sister Bernadette Madore, James O'Brien, attorney for the college, discovered that separate incorporation for AMC could easily be construed as the foundation of a *de novo* college. A new institution would be most unwelcome in an already crowded academic environment, where even colleges and universities with longer traditions and larger endowments than Anna Maria College now faced difficulty in a competitive market. Added to this, was the possible threat that AMC's degree-granting powers would be reduced from the existing broad base to a restrictive one of bachelor degrees only.

With this important information and with the help of legal counsel from AICUM (Association of Independent Colleges and Universities of Massachusetts) and other legal consultants, the board of trustees of the corporation, *The Sisters of St. Ann,* decided that AMC's needs and goals would be best served by restructuring the separate incorporation plan. To that end, the congregation of the Sisters of Saint Anne took steps to establish itself as a new cor-

Twenty-four newly-appointed trustees at their first meeting in 1980.

William V. Guerin, first lay chairperson of the Board of Trustees, 1981.

poration,[71] *The Community of the Sisters of Saint Anne*, and relinquished to Anna Maria College the 1887 corporation known as *The Sisters of St. Ann* with its existing charter and degree-granting powers. Anna Maria College remained for the congregation one of its prime apostolic interests. The relationship between the college and the congregation changed only insofar as the latter would no longer assume fiscal responsibility for the former. However, the congregation did not wish to diminish its commitment to Catholic higher education and would thus maintain a perspective on the mission of the college and continue to espouse the vision of the foundresses. The congregation, as sponsor of the institution, would be especially attentive to the religious dimension of the curriculum, campus ministry, student, faculty, and personnel services.

Concurrent with these activities, the president of the college, Sister Bernadette Madore, with the invaluable assistance of Richard A. Nelson, director of development and community affairs, assembled a cadre of twenty-four new trustees drawn from the local community, the commonwealth, and the nation.

Even before all the incorporation work was completed and all documents assembled, on October 21, 1979,[72] the group met with the incumbent board of trustees and the administrative officers of the college. Finally, on Sunday, April 13, 1980, a group of 24 newly-appointed trustees—15 lay persons; 7 Sisters of Saint Anne, 2 members of the clergy: Bishop Bernard J. Flanagan and Monsignor John F. Murphy—gathered for an historic meeting with the members of the incumbent board of trustees of the corporation, *The Sisters of St. Ann*. William V. Guerin; vice President of Kidder, Peabody, Inc. of Springfield, and Shirley M. Maguire, senior vice president of Freedom Federal Savings Bank, were appointed acting chairman and acting vice-chair of the board of trustees of the corporation, *The Sisters of St. Ann*. Hereby, the congregation dissolved all legal ties with the college and ceded to it, as a gift, 180.28 acres of land and all existing buildings. The assets between the college and the congregation were separated and, in the act of division, the Sisters of Saint Anne divested themselves of four million dollars of property and the college remained with a debt of $1,021,901 to the sisters. This debt was unsecured and non-interest-bearing. The new board included representatives from the medical profession, banking, investment banking, law, higher and secondary education, business, the arts, and politics.[73]

Separate incorporation of the college, new bylaws, development of role definitions for the officers of the college administration, selection of a 24-member board (including the president) required two years of intense study and activity. Anna Maria College found the new organizational structure effective. It delineated decision-making parameters for the board of trustees and the administration, providing policy-making for the former and operations functions for the latter. As expected, an NEASC evaluation team visited Anna Maria College on March 15-17, 1981. The following excerpts from an October 9, 1981 letter from the Commission on Institutions of Higher Education gave a foretaste of the results:

It is my pleasure to inform you that at its meeting on October 5, 1981, the Commission on Institutions of Higher Education voted to recommend to the Executive Committee of the New England Association of Schools and Colleges, Inc. that Anna Maria College be approved for continuing accreditation for a period of seven years....

The Commission has asked me to commend Anna Maria College for the significant strengthening of its governance and its much improved financial situation....

Final action on this recommendation was taken by the executive committee of NEASC at its meeting of December 10, 1981.

As early as 1979, in answer to NEASC's recommendation that the members of the faculty at Anna Maria College have a governance structure of their own, the faculty began to work on the concept of a Faculty Senate. Much time and effort were spent in organizing this body. In the fall of 1980, President Madore asked the senate

'THE FRIENDS OF ANNA MARIA COLLEGE'

*I*n the fifties, when I was growing up in Worcester, Anna Maria College was a household word. My mother, Gertrude Jacques, was one of the founders of the "Friends of Anna Maria College," a group of people eager to assist the young college. As such, she spent many years in service to the institution. She also served on the advisory board of the college and, during her long association with that group, developed a close friendship with Sister Irene Socquet. For the women in our family, after receiving primary and secondary education from the Sisters of Saint Anne, Anna Maria College was the institute of choice for pursuing higher learning.

— *Michele Jacques, S.S.A., Co-leader of St. Marie Province, 1993-1999*

Sr. Therese Noury (left) and Sr. Michele Jacques.

SSA COMMUNITY DAYS AT ANNA MARIA COLLEGE

*F*or many summers, the Anna Maria College campus hosted the Sisters of Saint Anne for their annual community days. These days were filled with various activities: spiritual, intellectual, and social. I remember how the large auditorium (now the Zecco Performing Arts Center), in Foundress Hall, would be a space for worship in the morning, a lecture hall in the afternoon, and an activities center in the evening.

I have fond memories of walks down Sunset Lane, picnics behind Socquet House near the pond, chats and snacks in the lounges of Madonna Hall, and overall good times! Above all, the friendly, welcoming atmosphere of the campus and the warmth of its people were the hallmark of these community days together.

— *Therese Noury, S.S.A., Co-leader of St. Marie Province, 1993-1999*

to begin functioning within its tentative constitution and bylaws in order to refine the organization further. On May 15, 1982, at a full board meeting, the trustees approved the senate document. The issue of governance, so long a matter for resolution, was now considered closed and patterns would evolve with changing needs. But in human affairs, hardly any issue is ever definitively closed; still it was gratifying that the necessary steps had been taken to insure that the college was governed according to the rubrics of the time. It was a happy and reassuring situation in light of what was taking shape on the horizon. New forces were at work which would eventually affect the very fabric of higher education.

The decade of the eighties began with a deepening global dread of nuclear annihilation. A tectonic shift, from a mass industrial to an information society, was occurring and its final impact promised to be more profound than the 19th century change from an agricultural to an industrial society. The information highway with its extraordinary capacity to transmit, sort, store, manage, or utilize knowledge and data extended the boundaries of education, adding a dynamic dimension to learning, teaching, collaboration, and research. It was also a vigorous force which stretched the fabric of Anna Maria College in most of its administrative, academic, physical, and student dimensions.

The college continued to reach beyond its traditional population, and soon its non-traditional students numbered close to a thousand. Classes met from early morning till 10:00 P.M. and the campus was bright with lights and activity far into the evening. The opportunities which the information highway presented to higher education seemed limitless. However, it was a two-edged sword with both opportunity and affordability requiring added consideration. The Anna Maria College community needed to develop more knowledge about this technology; to generate interest among faculty, staff, and students and to acquire the necessary resources to provide its availability. Divine Providence came to the rescue.

As part of its long-range plan, Anna Maria College took advantage of its eligibility for federal support under Title III. On January 19, 1981,[74] the college submitted a proposal written by Cecile Betit, assistant to the president. It was funded to the amount of $183,000 by the Department of Health, Education, and Welfare. Later, the grant was extended to September 30, 1985 and represented approximately $500,000 of equipment and development services to the institution. It strengthened five basic areas of its educational process: improvement of administrative capability and management; development of a computer science minor; instructional development; establishment of a career development center; and development of a student resource center. Through the improvement of administrative capability and the establishment of a computer science program, AMC hoped to approach the technological mainstream.

Technical assistance required for the organization of a computer science program came from the business world. Thomas Hourihan, vice president for human resources at the Norton Company in Worcester and a member of the board of trustees of the college, supplied the know-how. A well-developed and practical program was soon available to faculty and students making computer literacy at Anna Maria a possibility. Learning to use computers requires a mental skill which places it in an honorable position vis-a-vis the liberal arts which are, in essence, the arts of thinking and communicating. The first course in computer science was offered in September 1981 and by September 1982, more than 100 students had enrolled.

Again with Title III funds, NDSL (National Direct Student Loan) billing in the finance office was computerized. With the installation of an Apple II computer in the office of public affairs, the staff embarked on a new direction in work management. A very important innovation involved the electronic typesetting of the college catalog from the computer console in the public affairs office directly to the printer's shop. The cost of producing each page of the college catalog was reduced by 80 percent through this process. The importance of Title III funding for Anna Maria College cannot be overestimated. It added new dimensions to administrative, academic, and student life serving a crucial role on campus and making a significant and visible contribution to the strengthening of the college. The institution

A MEMORY SCROLL

I have many fond memories of my years at Anna Maria but one stands out in a special manner. In the fall of 1981, students, faculty, administration, and staff signed a scroll in a gesture of sympathy for the people of Egypt on the loss of Anwar Sadat, assassinated for his efforts to bring peace to the Near East.

Joseph Stango, Michel Lussier, and Keith Ciccone flew to Washington D.C. with public relations director, Phillip O'Brien, to present the scroll to Senator Edward M. Kennedy.

This gesture of sympathy from the college was the students' way of expressing their understanding of the peace efforts and their commitment to a just and peaceful world.

— *Hollie Ingraham, Dean of Students, 1978–1986*

Seated (left to right): Senator Edward Kennedy and Phillip O'Brien.
Standing (left to right): Joseph Stango '82, Michel Lussier '83, and Keith Ciccone '83.

Ground-breaking ceremony for Mondor-Eagen Library, July 1981.

society-transforming force. As the new age emerged, it was important for Anna Maria College and all institutions of higher learning to become flexible, technology literate, and more creative in the use of dynamic models of instruction.

At the same time, another major institutional accomplishment provided a dramatic and tangible dimension to the campus. After a long delay, the construction of the campus library was a special event and its relevance was enhanced immeasurably by the steps taken to establish the new computer technology. In the spring of 1980, the board of trustees voted to undertake a capital fund campaign with professional counsel, in view of building a long-needed library. After a feasibility study which took a few weeks, fund raising began in earnest and by the end of 1981 the campaign netted $1,118,000, of which $786,000 was in cash and $332,000, in pledges. Ground for the library was broken on July 29, 1981, and construction proceeded at a rapid pace, so that on April 16, 1982, most of the library holdings found a new place in the soft-colored, carpeted rooms of the Mondor-Eagen library. The floor space was quadrupled. This construction fulfilled the dream of the former presidents of the college and the hopes of the librarian, faculty, staff, and students. It was completely debt-free.[75] The most joyous event of the calendar year 1982 was, without doubt, the dedication of the library. It took place on September 25, 1982, a bright, crisp fall day, in the presence of both the first and second presidents of the college, the first registrar, the trustees, and members of the general and provincial administrations of the Sisters of Saint Anne who very generously contributed the largest gift to the capital fund campaign. Numerous other benefactors were in attendance along with alumni, friends, and the

was more self-assured and had a clearer focus on its future. It was Title III funding that permitted the advent of PCs (personal computers) on campus and the mounting interest in this dynamic technology which, even at this early stage, had an impact resembling that achieved by Gutenberg, in the field of communication.

Simultaneously, higher education executives began to sense the challenge in the intersection of the expanding educational potential of information technology and the mounting external pressure for more accountable and cost-effective instructional programs. The question was: what aspects of instruction and learning could best be delivered by the faculty and which by the new electronic technologies?

There was much to capture the attention of higher education in this dynamic technological dimension. However, at AMC as well as in many other colleges, the productivity payoff of the information superhighway would come only in the nineties with the domestication of the internet, improved PCs, and the web's arrival as a

campus community. The day was "Anna Maria College Day" as proclaimed by the town of Paxton. The Mondor-Eagen Library was named after the two women most responsible for founding the institution: the first president and the first registrar. It was dedicated through a symbolic act using an antiphonary from the cathedral of Leon in Spain, published in 1482, exactly 500 years before this dedication. The opening of this very ancient tome by William V. Guerin, chairman of the board, assisted by President Bernadette Madore, marked the formal opening and official dedication of the library.

It is interesting to note that on August 20, 1981, a few days before the ground-breaking, a letter from Joseph S. Hopkins, head-librarian of the Worcester Public Library, brought news of an opportunity for the library at Anna Maria College to be placed at the forefront of modern library technology and services. A grant of $700,000 was assured to the Worcester Public Library for the purchase of a computer to provide automated resource-sharing for public and academic libraries in central and western Massachusetts, provided a site could be found to locate this computer. Mr. Hopkins invited AMC to become the site, in its new library, for the computer, its operations, and other relevant functions. The college accepted to share some of its soon-to-be-acquired space and be part of this telecommunications system, owned by Central and Western Massachusetts Automated Resource System, known as C/W MARS. Through the use of the Online Computer Library Center, the AMC library was assured of a wealth of informational sources.

As a result of the services available in the new library and the instructional development afforded to faculty, staff, and students in the use of computers, modems, and electronic searches, faculty research activity increased. Some of the faculty initiated on-going research projects in their particular areas of expertise, and others delivered papers on campus or at national conferences, attesting to their research skills. Presenters were members of the departments of English, history, religious studies, and biology.

In accord with Anna Maria College's focus on meeting the learning needs of under-served populations, the college, upon request by the administration of Quincy Junior College offered, on the Quincy campus, a third and fourth year sequence of courses in business management. Accepting this invitation provided, for AMC, the opportunity to extend the benefits of its mission to a broader constituency; and, for Quincy, an attraction for potential students. Upon request by Dean Louise Soldani, NEASC granted approval and courses were offered as early as October 1982. The program *per se* was successful but the population which Quincy Junior College served was from a milieu where a major interest lay in developing trades as occupations. In spite

Interior of the newly dedicated Mondor-Eagen Library, 1982.

127

THE EXECUTIVE MBA
(Master's in Business Administration)

*W*hen the AMC Executive MBA, an intensive all-day Saturday program, was being offered at St. Elizabeth's Hospital in Boston it experienced phenomenal growth. One day the Hospital Administrator registered a complaint with me. Much to his chagrin, our faculty and students were almost completely taking over the parking lot every Saturday.

I told President Madore about the situation and she looked at me thoughtfully and said: "Isn't that the program everybody said couldn't possibly attract students?" I nodded. "Well," she said, "do you think you could fill some parking spaces here on campus on Saturdays?" This is how the Saturday Executive MBA program took root on the Paxton campus. St. Elizabeth's parking problems were resolved by moving the program to a consortium of sister hospitals—each offering a certain number of courses per semester. It was a win-win situation.

— *Francis R. Mazzaglia, D.Ed., Director of business programs, 1980-1985, Professor of business*

of the efforts of Quincy Junior's president and the willingness of Anna Maria College, the program endured for only a few years. This demise became an encouragement for AMC to extend its search for other groups in need of the education it had to offer.

New academic opportunities allowed the college to embrace other populations. One such opportunity presented itself in Worcester. In a gesture of cooperation, Anna Maria College offered two special programs during the academic year 1981-82. First, the biology department taught a three-credit course to biology honor students at Holy Name Central Catholic High School. Second, in the winter of 1982, twenty-six young men and women from Worcester area high schools, who stood to lose social security tuition benefits if they were not enrolled in a full-time college program by May 2, 1982, were offered a special full-semester beginning February 15, 1982. They registered for four three-credit courses at a reduced tuition rate. From both of these special programs, six students continued their post-secondary education at AMC. As results of a needs study within the business and nursing populations, two new programs, one in nursing and the other, an execu-

tive MBA, received approval and were enthusiastically received. The nursing program, originally spear-headed by Dean Soldani, established a working relationship with Memorial Hospital in Worcester. One course of this program was offered at the hospital site, and this cooperative endeavor facilitated by Dr. Sandra Rasmussen greatly favored the receipt of a $26,000 grant from the Rice Foundation for program development. The master's in nursing was transformed, in the early nineties, into an attractive graduate program which combined, for RNs seeking an advanced degree in administration, graduate business courses with offerings in health care administration. Dr. Francis Mazzaglia organized and tailored the executive MBA program to be an intensive, all-Saturday, closely structured program of study for highly motivated men and women who planned to pursue professional careers as executives. It consisted of nine-week sequences spaced by one free Saturday. It continued for over ten years when, because of some ill-advised substitution of courses from the regular MBA program, it lost its prestige and appeal and merged with the latter.

During this decade, the traditional population of students stretched the dimensions of its self-orientation. New societal and cultural forces resulting from the civil rights and Vietnam war protest movements influenced students and they became much more independent and pragmatic than former generations. These powerful forces also engendered a reluctance to accept many of society's traditions. True to its mission, the college accepted the students in their new self-orientation dimension and worked with them so that they

Students in the eighties. Standing to the far right, Hollie Ingraham, dean of students.

might become fully functional as moral human beings. Reasoned commitment to values; development of skills needed for making sound decisions; and moral activity in accord with these values and skills were three specific areas in which Anna Maria College, as a Catholic institution, attempted to assist the moral growth of its students. The vision and the mission of Anna Maria College emphasized the belief that moral behavior is a community matter, and that all the members subtly affect one another by the example of moral (or less-than-moral) behavior they represent.

There was continued proof that the Anna Maria student body was not an island untouched by the problems besetting American youth. For example, there had been ongoing discussion on most co-educational campuses concerning the length and control of parietals in college residences. The case of parietals was never completely closed. It gained momentum in the late sixties and early seventies when most unisex colleges became co-educational. The college president placed the issue of parietals within a philosophical context in a statement found in the college catalog:

It is imperative that the student attending or planning to attend AMC be committed to a philosophy of education that rests on a value system fostering not only the intellectual but also the personal growth of the student.... The college attempts to create a campus climate that encourages freedom from pressure to conform, and provides space and time for privacy, for quiet reflection, for serious and undisturbed study. The creation of such an atmosphere requires a sincere consideration of life in the residence hall. It definitely precludes the concept of "open" housing...all humans, students or not, need certain periods of time in their lives in which to be alone with themselves and their thoughts....Again, to be free requires, among other things, that space—physical, intellectual psychological, and spiritual—be safeguarded and inviolable at all times....

Dynamic forces such as those described above coalesced to place Anna Maria College squarely on a path which, while leading to greater excellence, would be fraught with unexpected demands on its vigor and courage as a maturing institution.

"How does AMC strive for authentic excellence?"

XIII

A CHALLENGE TO ACADEMIC EXCELLENCE & MORE OPPORTUNITIES

*I*n the academic year 1983-84, President Bernadette Madore appointed a task force called "On the Search for Excellence" whose charge was to examine conditions affecting the development of the college. These conditions included factors such as the local and regional economy, government policies and regulations, demographics, the changing ratios of minorities in the American population, and regional shifts to high technology and service. The historical mission of Anna Maria College, its traditions, values, and ethos all received in-depth consideration. The question was always: "How does AMC strive for authentic excellence?"

The members of the task force were: Carol Williams, Sr. Paulette Gardner, Joseph Wilson, and Brian Mitchell. They identified economic trends and directions, societal changes, population goals—all of which, if given positive collaborative response, would place the college in a favorable position to serve future constituencies.

In the fall semester of 1984, to formulate its final report, the task force focused attention on three main questions:

1. How can institutional programs be adapted efficiently to match the learning demands of new student populations?
2. How can existing institutional resources be utilized creatively to support new programs as well as new roles for faculty?
3. In light of the challenge of new missions,
   a) what contributions can be made to the understanding of moral conduct and its implementation on and off campus?
   b) what facilities can be provided to enhance the cultural life of surrounding communities?

In March 1985, the task force completed its work[76] and the faculty and administration listened intently to the recommendations offered for immediate and future application. The maturing effect of this study on the academic community can be attributed to the work done by the task force and the discussions it sparked across the campus among students, staff, faculty, and administrators. It was the basis for coping with a problem which had not previously confronted Anna Maria College.

In March 1985,[77] one of Anna Maria College's programs was sharply criticized for academic inadequacies by an investigative team of *The Boston Globe*. Although the college objected to what it termed major inaccuracies in stories originating in *The Globe*, the unmistakable motive was to denigrate the criminal justice program and other AMC programs as well. The college cooperated with the reporters, prepared a response, but was deeply disappointed by the results when the truth was blatantly ignored.

President Madore appointed a Blue Ribbon Commission to establish a model curriculum for part-time graduate programs in criminal justice. In addition, she also assembled a special campus committee to conduct an internal audit of the graduate division, particularly of the criminal justice program which was under attack.

An editorial appeared in the July 19 edition of the *Worcester Telegram*. It came as a relief to all who supported and understood Anna Maria College:

A STRONG RESPONSE

In March, Anna Maria College's criminal justice program was sharply criticized for academic inadequacies said to be shared with similar programs at Northeastern University in Boston and New Hampshire College in Hooksett, N.H.

Anna Maria officials objected to what they called major inaccuracies in the stories originated by The Boston Globe. *More important they decided to tighten up the program.*

College President Bernadette Madore established a blue-ribbon panel chaired by former state Attorney General Robert H. Quinn, who was a sponsor of the 1970 legislation that set up the Police Pay Incentive Program. That program enables police personnel to boost their pay by as much as 25 to 30 percent by completing a master's program. Others on the Anna Maria commission were James G. Reardon, a Worcester lawyer; John Ryan, director of the Worcester Consortium for Higher Education; Halstead Taylor, retired Worcester police chief; Philip J. Vairo, president of Worcester State College; and state representative Thomas White.

The changes recommended by the panel should answer some of the criticisms. Appointment of Robert L. Zukowski as full-time director of the program will give the college closer control and supervision. Some of the academic recommendations will give the Anna Maria degree more prestige.

The degree is not one for academics who intend to pursue careers in research on criminal justice and law enforcement. It is a program designed especially for working police personnel with a special emphasis on the skills needed for that work. A greater emphasis on management training will benefit the participants and the taxpayers by improving management and supervisory skills in the state's police departments. The added monitoring will help Anna Maria keep the program on track academically and professionally.

All in all, despite the injustices Anna Maria felt were done it by the March reports, the college and its criminal justice program should be stronger because of the vigorous action Sister Madore and the administration took to meet the charges.

The Alumni were kept informed of the steps the college took regarding this program and the response was supportive. The campus community, already strengthened by the zeal of the task force on "The Search for Excellence" whose report was still being studied by administration and faculty, responded with optimism.

In effect, the Blue Ribbon Commission weighed the fundamental question of what type of program was most appropriate for Anna Maria College. The members agreed that a graduate program in criminal justice should clearly reflect an interdisciplinary approach. The curriculum should recognize the interdependence of cultural norms, traditions, value systems, and social responses to problem solving. It should also provide for the study and analysis of social goals and their relationship to government policy. Approached in this manner, the program's mission became clearly consistent with that of the college which is to foster social awareness and dedication to peace and justice.

The internal evaluation committee, appointed by the president, conducted an audit of all programs in the graduate division. Entrance requirements, curricula, instructional practices, evaluation of students and faculty, and research opportunities were scrutinized and upgraded where necessary. Full-time directors were appointed to chair each graduate program. Their responsibilities included marketing and enrollment management; services to student, faculty, and off-campus sites when applicable. Site administrators were also designated at each off-campus location. In addition, under the direction of the dean of the graduate division, external advisory boards were established to monitor the programs. These actions gave each graduate program more credibility and identified the graduate division as an important element in the fulfillment of the mission of the college.

Another population of adults enjoyed the benefits of an Anna Maria College education. In January 1984, after the submission of a successful proposal to the Massachusetts National Guard for the granting of a bachelor of business degree by Anna Maria College, and the approval of NEASC, members of the National Guard joined the ranks of AMC students at four sites within the state. Their purpose was to heed governmental stipulations which gave preference for advancement to holders of baccalaureate degrees.

OFF-CAMPUS INSTRUCTION

*O*ff-campus instruction was carried out under the supervision of local site coordinators. However, we soon discovered that continuing high quality instruction depends upon regular visitation by central academic administrators. In addition to encouraging acceptable standards of instruction, the presence of officials from Paxton gave students and teachers alike a sense of belonging to the Anna Maria community and helped strengthen a nascent loyalty that otherwise might have waned. As vice-president of the college, I visited all off-campus classes frequently and unannounced. I can attest not only to generally sound instruction and lively student participation but also to a remarkable feeling of commitment exhibited by part-time older students, many of whom had never set foot on the Paxton campus. This steadily expanding reservoir of support generated by the yearly addition of grateful graduates from the extended education programs strengthens the college's favorable recognition throughout the region.

— *Charles M. Hepburn, Ph.D.,*
Vice-president for academic and student affairs, 1985-1991

THE NATIONAL GUARD PROGRAM

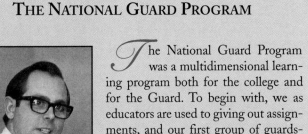

*T*he National Guard Program was a multidimensional learning program both for the college and for the Guard. To begin with, we as educators are used to giving out assignments, and our first group of guardsmen, being superior officers, was also very used to giving out orders. Right away we had too many people in charge. However, once our program got under way, it was a pleasant and mutually beneficial experience culminating in Anna Maria College's only December graduation.

— *Richard L. Connors, Professor of psychology*

On December 8, 1985, eighty members of the Massachusetts National Guard received their degrees (BBA) at commencement exercises held on campus in the large auditorium at Foundress Hall. The 215th Army Band greatly enhanced the ceremony with impeccable renditions of musical selections and choral numbers. Families and friends were in attendance for this premier event. It was one of the warmest graduation ceremonies witnessed at Anna Maria College.

English as a Second Language (ESL) received much attention on campus. Students coming from several foreign countries, especially Japan, received assistance in the assimilation and use of the English language. The most dramatic and significant academic improvement in meeting their learning needs was an innovation in the delivery of instruction. Individualization provided a superior alternative to conventional lecture-style teaching and met each student on personal terms. Each student's program was tailored to personal career goals, interest, and cultural exposure. The acquisition and effective exercise of traditional language skills in listening, speaking, reading, and writing require clear cultural understanding and were greatly enhanced by social and cultural components.

Thus, growth and development of the ESL program reflected non-academic as well as academic pursuits. The awareness and interest of American students were enhanced by the establishment of an International Center sponsored by the Student Government Association. Sister Pauline Madore, as director of the ESL program, not only visited Japan for recruitment, but she dedicated much time and energy to the instruction of the foreign students and to their overall well-being. She served as teacher, chauffeur, counselor, confidante, and liaison for the host and hospitality program which integrated foreign students in host families and greatly hastened their acculturation. The ESL program, in its execution, was an ideal fulfillment of the mission of the college in practically all of its essentials.

Sr. Pauline Madore, director of ESL (English as a Second Language) in the late eighties.

International Club, standing on the left, Sr. Pauline Madore.

came from as near as Paxton and as far away as California and Colorado. They were treated to topics including "Freedom in American Life" and "World War II Literature" on campus, and "A Study of American Art" at the Worcester Art Museum. Afternoon activities included a bridge tournament, trivial pursuit challenges, nature walks, low-impact aerobics, and stress management. There were trips to Higgins Armory, the New England Science Center, the Worcester Historical Society, and to Old Sturbridge Village. Elderhostel is an international program for participants, age 60 or above. It was highly successful in creating good public relations and a heightened awareness of the college.

With new, more diverse populations enrolling at the college, it was an increasing challenge to create a campus where international, non-traditional, disabled, handicapped, and minority students could learn in the same educational environment. It was necessary for administration and faculty to be aware of issues vital to the education of these students and to prepare curricula and pedagogical strategies adapted to their needs. A committee on recruitment and retention of students from multiple cultures and racial groups was appointed by the president. The purpose was to develop and strengthen the college's relationship to a multicultural community and to sensitize the campus to the needs of a multicultural student population. Years ago, the nation was known as a "melting pot" but now the ideal was more a "stew pot," connoting not a loss, but a retention of cultural identity.

In the summer of 1988, Dr. Charles M. Hepburn, vice president for academic and student affairs, spearheaded an Elderhostel program on campus. It attracted twenty-five elderly applicants who

At this time, the education department, while being an enabler, was exceptionally successful in its service to older populations and in the fulfillment of its mission. Because as many as 10,000 new teachers would be needed within the next five years, Anna Maria College reactivated its graduate program in education and directed it

International Students, 1989.

MEMORIES FROM MACAU, CHINA

*F*ive years at AMC brought me a lot of unforgettable experiences and so I will just let my heart lead me as I write. I arrived at AMC in the winter of 1987—a very cold and snowy winter. As I entered the campus of AMC, I did not know how I should feel. The campus was quiet and peaceful. I felt excited as I saw snow all over the campus. It was the first time I ever saw snow in all my life, but also the first time I ever went to a foreign country all by myself. With that thought sadness set in and my heart sank. I did not know a single soul here in the U.S., and I was almost 25 hours away from home—by plane. That night I could not sleep. I completely surrendered to fear and loneliness.

The following morning as I went to the window and scrolled up the shade in my room, I could not believe my eyes. It was not just snow, but inches of snow. Even the cars were buried in the snow. I decided to go outside to feel what snow was really like. It was bitter cold for me who came from a place where the temperature never goes below 50 degrees. On my way to the cafeteria, I met a lady in her fifties. When she saw me, she came up to me without any hesitation, and said: "Oh, my dear, this is Paxton. You have to dress warmly, you know." As she spoke, she reached out and zipped up my jacket for me. All of a sudden I felt less strange with the place as if I already knew someone from there. She was the first friend I made at AMC, and she was Sister Pauline Madore.

— *Alice Fong-Chan (bachelor's, 1990; master's, 1992)*

to liberal arts graduates who wanted to be elementary school teachers, but who had no formal training in education. Regulations, approved by the state board of education in December 1986, made it possible for people who matriculated in this program to teach while they completed their education courses. The board's creation of the status of " apprentice teacher" was intended to streamline the teacher certification process. Students who enrolled full-time at Anna Maria in the new twelve-month program were eligible for a master's degree in one year.

The education department also collaborated with the Coolidge school in Shrewsbury to create a professional development school model. The education department staff of the college and of the Coolidge school spent two years on this plan, which was presented before the Massachusetts Field Center for Teaching and Learning at the University of Massachusetts in Boston. The model, chosen from a field of fourteen, was

selected for an implementation grant of $10,000 as a prototype of future teacher training.

The years 1986 and 1987 also witnessed important celebrations on campus. Anna Maria College celebrated its fortieth anniversary in 1986 and, in 1987, the campus marked the bicentennial of the United States Constitution.

To relive the history of the college, there were four series of exhibits in the Socquet House board room, presenting photos and memorabilia of the college from 1946 through the 1980s. On Sunday, April 27, 1986, the college, in a Town/Gown ceremony, commemorated its arrival in Paxton and the establishment of one of those unique town/gown relationships—the kind that does not happen in every college town. It was a gesture of appreciation to the town that welcomed the college and helped it grow from a fledgling college to a coeducational institution boasting over 1500 students. The two-hour ceremony culminated in the release of bright bal-

Celebrating the Bicentennial

at Anna Maria College

Top: Members of the Rutland Militia give the concluding musket salute.
Left: Singing of "America the Beautiful" by Donna Varney.
Bottom left: The plaque over the time capsule.
Bottom right: Some items within the capsule.

loons in the clearing blue sky. Anna Maria College honored four Paxton residents who had done much to help the college become an integral and permanent part of the town community. Bishop Timothy J. Harrington called the four town residents "the embodiment of the spirit of the New England neighbors who helped Anna Maria College carry on its mission." Also honored were four women, Sisters of Saint Anne, who had been associated with the college since its early days.[78]

The town of Paxton designated April 23, Anna Maria College Day, marking the founding of the college in Marlboro in 1946. In an editor-

INTERNATIONAL WEEK AT AMC

Mutsumi Ishitate (left) '92 and Maureen Villars '93.

*M*y best memory of AMC is "International Week." We asked professors and administrators to don the various traditional costumes of the foreign students and they went to classes and offices attired in native dress of all kinds. It was fun and brought International and American students closer.

In addition to a degree in business, my most valuable possessions from AMC are strong friendships. There, I became a caring, understanding, and friendly person. I used to be a shy girl who could not raise her hand in class. At AMC, sisters, students, and teachers were very open and helpful. In a relatively short time, I knew almost everyone on campus. It was great! People cared about me. In turn, I cared about them. Maureen Villars from Ghana, Africa, became my best friend. Even though I live in Japan we still e-mail each other. I would like to say "thank you" to Anna Maria College.

— *Mutsumi Ishitate, Class of 1992*

GHANA, AFRICA TO PAXTON, U.S.A.

*M*y AMC experience started when I encountered a Japanese student, Mutsumi Ishitate. I met Sumi at Holy Names College in Oakland, CA. She was on an exchange program and I was in dire straits— on the verge of being kicked out of school because I could not afford the fees. I spoke to Sumi about my situation and she suggested that Anna Maria College might be more affordable and also might offer me a scholarship. Sumi said that the person I wanted to speak to was the late Sr. Pauline Madore. I did as advised, sent my transcripts and within 3 months, I was an accepted student at Anna Maria College with two scholarships: Presidential and Pincus-Madore. Life was looking good again.

I finally reached Paxton. A young student from Ghana in West Africa who had found Oakland, CA cold in June. Here I was in Paxton, MA in September anxious and yet waiting to experience my first snow. The students had a ball with my fears and concerns. They told me about blizzards, snow storms that completely covered cars, white-out conditions, fire alarms that went off on cold nights when students were taking a shower....I was honestly concerned that if I walked too slowly outdoors, I might freeze in my tracks and become a pillar of salt like Lot's wife! I survived it all. Sister Pauline was the ski pole in my life—not strong enough to prevent me from falling, but available, reliable, ever present, and ready to lend an ear. Anna Maria College was my Alma Mater in the true sense of the word. It is a place one can never forget. Even though I graduated several years ago, it is the one place where I still take all my guests.

— *Maureen Villars, Class of 1993*

Architect's concept of the Fuller Activities Center.

ial, *The Catholic Free Press*, April 25, 1986, expressed congratulations:

> *That Anna Maria College in Paxton is forty years old this year may surprise many area people. To them, Anna Maria is still the fledgling college, its campus newly transferred to a diocese newly established. Yet, it was as long ago as 1946 and as seemingly far away as Marlboro when Anna Maria registered its first students. Making use, temporarily, of the facilities of Saint Anne Academy, opened in 1888, the Sisters of Saint Anne relocated the burgeoning college in Paxton six years later. What had transpired in that six year interval was the coming into being, almost as if it were already full grown, of the diocese of Worcester. Displaying a confidence of which only the very young or the very mature are capable, the diocese under the energetic and imaginative Bishop John J. Wright, grew apace with the college. More than that, the development of the one in those days and in the intervening decades was fostered by the good fortune of the other ....Telling the story of this college which has long come into its own cannot be done without such an account recalling the input, beginning with human input, of the diocese and the outcome by way of manifold blessings poured out on Worcester county. The biography of the diocese of Worcester is the life story of Anna Maria graduates giving of themselves as teachers and technicians, through their talents and training, in as many areas of service as there are needs to be served. While the biography begins there, it does not end there. The contributions of the administration and the faculty, the students and alumni have gone beyond campus and have become county-wide and, indeed, country-wide. To Anna Maria, a happy fortieth and a still more prosperous future!*

On May 10, 1986, the college dedicated its new $1.5 million Fuller Activities Center for which ground was broken on September 28, 1985. The ceremony included the unveiling of a plaque acknowledging the generosity of the George F. and Sybil H. Fuller Foundation of Worcester. Some of the participants in the ceremony were Richard Bullock, president and chief executive officer of Wyman-Gordon Company and chairman of the college's capital fund campaign; Richard C. Caparso, chairman of the board of trustees of Anna Maria College; Russell Fuller, treasurer of the Fuller Foundation; Worcester Mayor John D. Anderson; and Christian Baehrecke, Paxton selectman.

TRUSTEESHIP IN THE EIGHTIES

*T*he strategy of the board of trustees to address programs structured to meet the demanding challenges of the eighties was centered around a communal philosophy. Strong commitment from trustees, administrators, faculty, staff, and students was required. The task of trustees was to establish priorities, goals, and plans to achieve acceptable results. Our theme was: "Plan and Work — Work the Plan!" Responsibility and accountability became benchmarks as we monitored and measured our performance in fiscal matters and institutional objectives. We set up communication routes in all directions so that the campus community was fully informed. We encouraged input from all areas with proper feed-back. We promoted "Humanagement" treating all with respect and dignity. Success crowned our efforts and, in addition, we had fun. It was one of the most rewarding periods of my life!

— Richard B. McNamara, Chairman of the Board of Trustees, 1986-1988
Trustee, 1983-1988

On September 17, 1987,[79] at 11 A.M., Anna Maria College marked, in a special ceremony, the bicentennial of the United States Constitution. The event was held on the campus rotary, where a time capsule was buried. Artifacts included in

J. Richard Bullock, chairman of the Capital Campaign for Fuller Activities Center.

the capsule were contributed by the college community, the Paxton school, historical commission, churches, and selectmen. It will be opened 50 years hence, in 2037. The program began with the singing of the national anthem, followed by an invocation by the chaplain and words of welcome by the president of the college. Massachusetts Senator Thomas P. White gave the official address. Most Reverend Bernard J. Flanagan, former bishop of Worcester and member of the board of trustees, gave the benediction which was followed by the singing of "America the Beautiful." Members of the Rutland militia gave the concluding musket salute. Richard B. McNamara, chairman of the board of trustees, presided at a special luncheon held in the Fuller Activities Center. It was an occasion to be long-remembered by the 200 people who viewed the ceremony on that bright September day, the one on which, two hundred years before, the final draft of the United States Constitution was approved in Philadelphia. This special event was Anna Maria College's way of celebrating what had come to be the oldest working constitution in the world, and it excited the minds of the students present, raising their consciousness to the document that is our trust.

Both celebrations—the fortieth anniversary and the marking of the bicentennial of the U.S. Constitution—raised among the participants social awareness and sensitivity to the sometimes heroic acts of our forbears who made possible the political and legal privileges we enjoy today.

From 1986 to 1988, the college prepared for a decennial evaluation by NEASC (New England

ONE GRADUATION I WILL NEVER FORGET

*O*ne year, the graduation committee asked that I make arrangements for a graduating music major to sing the National anthem, which I did.

Graduation day arrived. I made sure the vocalist, her keyboard accompanist, and I were on the stage at the right time. I asked the audience to stand for the singing of the National Anthem. As the duo was about to perform, I saw a cord fall from the electronic keyboard. The musician reattached the wire. I relaxed as the introduction was played again. Once more, the plug fell out. I stiffened. The accompanist reattached the plug one more time. There was a new beginning. I breathed a little easier as synthesizer and voice soared harmoniously.

Somewhere in the middle of the Anthem, I watched in terror as the keyboard again rejected the same cord. The accompaniment stopped, but the vocalist, mercifully continued. The plug was reconnected, not inconspicuously, and the music blended in with the vocalist once again. I became worried as the part in the Anthem was approaching when the vocalist had to hit high "C." Just then, the plug plopped out and the keyboard died. Blood pounded to my head. "Will she, can she do it alone?" I mumbled with dry mouth. The answer was as clear as her high C.

She finished. It was over. I hugged her as I would a returning hero. She left the stage to an instantaneous, standing ovation. I left vowing to look seriously into another career.

— Henry V. Rudin, Director of public affairs, 1987-1996

From left to right: Henry V. Rudin, Lauro F. Cavazos, U.S. Secretary of Education, Bishop Timothy J. Harrington, and Laura A. McGuire '90.

Graduate students at commencement, 1989.

lege....The academic identity, distinctiveness, we believe, and a major strength of Anna Maria College is in its offering of professional programs in a solid liberal arts context, i.e., with the core curriculum. It is this mission which gives Anna Maria its special niche—a role among colleges....Planning has been a major effort at Anna Maria College over a number of years. It is clear that planning has been a priority for the president. Clearly the college has invested considerable time and effort in the last twelve years in long-range planning and evaluation and there is considerable evidence to suggest that the plans have been used in guiding and evalu-

Association of Schools and Colleges). The accreditation review took place November 13-16, 1988. Dr. Paul Reiss, president of Saint Michael's College, chaired an especially good team. The exit interview was conducted before the entire college faculty and staff. A few weeks later, the president received a copy of the written report including the points made at the open session. On the 28th of April, President Bernadette Madore and Vice President Charles M. Hepburn appeared before the Commission of Higher Education at the Marriott Hotel in Worcester. A few days later, Dr. Charles Cook called Sister Bernadette Madore to announce that the college had been granted a ten-year accreditation. This came as welcome news. Dr. Paul Reiss,[80] chairman of the evaluation team, commented that:

Anna Maria College is to be commended and congratulated for its dedication to its self-study...." He adds: We, the team, were impressed by the openness, the friendliness of all, the willingness to share information and perspectives with us....The mission statement of Anna Maria College clearly reflects the history and values of the col-

*Mother and daughter,
Gloria '55 and Denise '88 Hand.*

142

Graduation, 1988.

faculty, together with members of the administration, act as a collegial team in the service of the students. Faculty appear to be supportive colleagues to each other....There does not seem to be the conflict of factions which often seems to affect other institutions.

The campus community rejoiced over the success of the evaluation and was especially proud of the ten-year accreditation. The decade ended in a flourish of events that had international repercussion. The Berlin Wall tumbled and the Soviet empire collapsed. Communism was on "the ash heap of history" as President Reagan had predicted in 1982.

The information superhighway, a dream and a hope in the early 80s, was already under construction on many campuses. Turning the calendar back a decade earlier emphasized major differences between the appearance of the campus and the present day-to-day world. In the closing year of the decade of the 80s, computers and fax machines, auto-dialers on telephones, microwaves, CD players, and VCRs were in general use. The library already harbored a state-of-the-art computer center.

Anna Maria College, in its mission statement, claims that its goal is not merely to promote intellectual excellence, but also to promote human excellence, a much more comprehensive and demanding ideal. The following chapter is the story of a non-academic venture within the college which remains a vital part of the mosaic, one involving total human development.

ating the development of the college....We would like to commend the college for the fine collegial spirit which pervades the organization... faculty and staff appear to be appropriately involved in the governance of the college.... We congratulate the college on the development of the several undergraduate programs....The dedication of the faculty of Anna Maria College to the students was one of the most impressive findings of the team's visit....We also found that the

"...Even in finally losing, barely, to a bigger team from a much larger school, the AMCats won."

— President William Dill

XIV

A PERSPECTIVE ON ATHLETICS

*T*he mission of the athletic department at AMC, which is to promote an interest in physical well-being and recreational exercise among students, and to help them grow in teamwork, esprit-de-corps, leadership, and maturity, is in keeping with the mission and goals of the college.

On October 11, 1978, one year after the appointment of the first director of athletics, Stephen Washkevich, Sandy Burgin, of *The Worcester Telegram*, wrote the following article describing the fortunes of the AMC field hockey team:

Last week, Anna Maria, in only its second varsity field hockey game, beat Rivier College of Nashua, N.H., 2-0, for the first "home" victory in any sport. Ironically, two days earlier Anna Maria was a 2-0 victim of Clark University which was winning its first field hockey game, but in its second year after a full season of losing... first year coach Cheryl St. Onge said:

Steven Washkevich, athletic director, 1977-1997.

#20 Andre Rheault reaching for the ball, Men's Basketball 1987-1988.

We had quite a celebration....The word of our victory spread over the campus almost as soon as the final whistle blew...some of the hurdles that we've had to overcome just to field a team really inspired the team to play perhaps above and beyond its capabilities.

In early August the yet-to-be Anna Maria field hockey team didn't even have a field to practice on. There was a good size tract of land which could perhaps accommodate a playing field, but there was a good size willow tree almost in the middle of what would be the field.

There were those, including second-year athletic director, Stephen Washkevich...who wanted to have the tree cut down to make room for the field. But there were the nuns and other administrators who didn't wish to tamper with Mother Nature and want-

ed the tree, somehow preserved. A compromise was struck and it was agreed that the tree would be transplanted. And so by late August the willow tree had found a new home near the dormitories and the land was cleared for a new field....

For those people who didn't even know Anna Maria had a field hockey team or even a sports program at all, take note. There are 22 sports activities, including intramurals offered at the "college on the hill" in Paxton. There are women's basketball and softball teams, a men's soccer team and plans for a men's basketball team this winter....

Steve Washkevich worked earnestly at establishing a competitive athletic program for both women and men. With plenty of fields for expansion and no further need for willow trees to look

STARTING THE ATHLETIC PROGRAM

To get the program started, I knew I had to develop a relationship with the students on a recreational basis. Team leaders and I took thirteen students up to the White Mountains for the weekend. We tobogganed in the moonlight all night long. We cooked and cleaned together. It was another step in getting the program off the ground. I remember taking twenty-two students overnight up Monadnock Mountain. We had one screen house for all of us. We did not sleep at all but the relationship kept on growing.

— *Stephen Washkevich, first athletics director, 1977–1997*

for new roots, he began resolutely to make a dent in the world of intercollegiate sports. Some excellent athletes joined the men's and women's teams until the director could say, in truth, that the athletics program was improving the image, reputation, and accrued value of the college. In the academic year, 1982-83, the program included the fielding of seven varsity teams, competing for the first time on a Division III level of the NCAA (National Collegiate Athletic Association).

The academic year 1984-85 began with the dedication of Caparso field which was named in honor of the parents of the chairman of the board, Richard C. Caparso. It represented a great asset in sustaining the attitude and improving the play of both the field hockey and soccer teams. It was also a great image builder and an opportunity to be good neighbors to the townspeople who often use the facility. The field was 335 feet long and 200 feet wide and was marked off at dimensions of 300 feet by 150 feet for field hockey.

In the summer of 1985, through donations from the Doehla Foundation, and the administration and staff of AMC, the athletic director

FIRST GAME IN FULLER CENTER

I can remember the first game we played in the Fuller Activities Center. It was a game never to be forgotten. We had a very large crowd and after all the hoopla of the dedication we played Worcester State (an excellent team) and beat them on a long shot at the buzzer! It was a good omen—better things were to come.

— *Stephen Washkevich,*
athletics director, 1977–1997

AN EXCITING TRUSTEESHIP

*M*y service to Anna Maria College was an exciting time of change, growth, and development at the college and in higher education in general. In my tenure as chairman of the board of trustees, the college completed the Fuller Activities Center, the Zecco Performing Arts Center, and the total restoration of the chapel.

It was my personal pleasure to donate the Caparso Field. My twelve-year association with Anna Maria College and President Madore was truly a satisfying and rewarding part of my life.

— *Richard C. Caparso, trustee 1980-1986; 1987-1993, Chairman of the Board (4 terms)*

installed a Fitness Trail. This facility was a well-balanced fitness system that added total body conditioning and cardiovascular monitoring to jogging. The system was composed of exercise stations located at intervals along a jogging trail.

From the founding of the athletic department in the academic year 1977-78 to the mid-eighties, home games took place in rented or "friendly" facilities. The level of energy, enthusiasm, and dedication required to pursue the development of the teams under such conditions cannot be over-estimated. At last, on September 28, 1985, at the time of the annual meeting of the board of trustees, official groundbreaking for an activities center was scheduled. It was dedicated on May 10, 1986, in the presence of the trustees, college community, alumni, friends, and members of the campaign cabinet, chaired by J. Richard Bullock, president

The Anna Maria Softball Team, 1981.

Men's Basketball, 1993.

#20 Carrie Hurley going for the basket, 1993.

of Wyman-Gordon. During the ceremony, present and former athletic captains and Sr. Irene Leblanc, whose submission of "AMCat" won the contest to name the mascot, unveiled a mural of the Anna Maria AMCat. The mural was designed by Danny Roy '83 and executed by Sally Graves '86 and Cathy Clark '86. To recognize a major contribution to the capital fund campaign by the Fuller Foundation, the activities center bore its name. With access to the quality facilities available and with the hiring of a full-time intramural director/athletic trainer, the intramural activities showed a more extensive growth in the academic year 1986-87. The department held memberships in the Commonwealth Coast Conference, the National Collegiate Athletic Association, the Eastern Collegiate Athletic Conference, the Massachusetts Association Intercollegiate Athletics for Women, the Women's Basketball Association, the New England Basketball Coaches Association, the Worcester Area Coaches Sportscasters and Sportswriters Association, and the New England Collegiate Athletic Conference.[81]

The department of athletics had a strong outreach to the community at large. During school vacations, local children used the activities center. The town of Paxton conducted karate and aerobic classes there. Some events held in the Center favored special olympics, teams from Friendly House, Central New England soccer camp, and basketball camps. The teams were encouraged to do public service; the men's basketball team visited hospitals during the holidays. They raised $700, through a raffle, to assist a child who was comatose following an accident. The AMCat Booster Club, established in the fall of 1987, raised dollars, generated interest, and sponsored events to promote the department. It financed the annual athletics awards banquet and purchased fertilizer for the fields, as well as plaques and banners for the champion teams. With time, the athletic program received excellent press coverage proving that success breeds success.

On March 2, 1996,[82] the college magazine *Visions* told an exciting and unique story of how the "AMCats Clawed Their Way to a NCAA Sweet 16" in these terms:

OF A PIG AND A BULL ON ALUMNI FIELD

Sr. Anita Poudrier watches the visiting pig on Alumni Field.

*A*lumni field attracted not only athletes but other characters who claimed it as their space at some time. On one occasion a large pig wandered on the field from an adjoining farm and had to be enticed off the premises by a banana tied to the end of a long pole. Sister Irene Socquet, a farm girl in her youth, finally succeeded in urging it back to its farm while the athletes loudly cheered her on—and the pig also! Another day, a bull paid a visit to the campus. Margaret Foskett, the switchboard operator, announced over the P.A. system, during the lunch hour, that a bull was on the loose in Alumni Field and urged students not to 'challenge the bull.' Of course, the cafeteria emptied immediately as all the students ran out to see the bull!

— *Stephen Washkevich,*
athletics director, 1977-1997

..Winless in its only four previous post-season appearances, the AMC's men's basketball team, sporting a 25-4 record and a 9 game winning streak, emerged from the 3rd seed in the northeast regional conference and rocketed into the Sweet 16 of the NCAA Division 3 Championship as they beat Babson 111-90 and then overcame a nine point second half deficit to shock favored Salem State (ranked 7th nationally) propelling them into the NCAA Division III Atlantic Sectionals. No small feat....

On March 9, an Atlantic Sectionals matchup against Stockton State College, in New Jersey, brought a loss to the AMCats. Interim President William Dill on March 18, 1996, gave his impression of the events surrounding this climax as follows:

...Even in finally losing, barely, to a bigger team from a much larger school, the AMCats won. Ten players, well coached on operating as a team so that it hardly mattered which five were on the floor, impressed everyone with their spirit, style, and talent. The sports editor from Babson put it well: "Anna Maria left the Babson players and supporters dazed and confused after forty minutes of spectacular basketball. Anna Maria played flawlessly and executed a perfect game plan.

But AMC won too. No more questions about: "Where's our school spirit?" Students, parents, staff and their families, alumni, and friends from the community found it and put it on display. The Babson reporter wrote that walking into the Anna

ATHLETIC HOME FIELDS

With the Fuller Activities Center the athletic program continued to grow. Baseball and softball were now in focus. Neither program had a home field on which to play. The word got out (on purpose) that we were looking for some help with a participatory low cost way of developing two sections of land for softball and baseball/soccer fields. A parent heard our plea and encouraged other parents to get involved and we ended up building both fields at no cost to the college. The Rutland Youth Soccer team was using our fields and volunteered help. On one Saturday about 100 boys and their parents raked stones and debris from both fields. We spread the seed ourselves with money from the AMCat Booster Club. Another parent donated all the infield dirt needed for both fields. The telephone company donated 10 full-size poles that were installed by the Paxton Light Company to serve as a backstop for the baseball field. We used fencing from the old tennis courts to complete the backstop. The field turned out better than expected. Other colleges called to use the field after the first year of use. The two fields are now some of the better fields in the area. The bonus was that the outfield of the baseball field served as a second soccer field.

— *Stephen Washkevich, athletics director, 1977-1997*

Maria gym was like walking into the movie HOOSIERS. Our hosts at Salem State and Rowan in New Jersey were amazed at how we turned out and cheered.

...Let's bottle some of the March Madness school spirit for new occasions in the weeks ahead. Let's not retreat to a "small college" mentality and surrender the gains in visibility and reputation that the AMCats achieved for us. They have reminded us that, in very large measure, we can become whatever we set our minds and hearts to be.

Reaching the SWEET 16 was indeed a great tribute to a talented and dedicated coaching staff led by Coach Paul Phillips and especially to athletic director, Stephen Washkevich, who had experienced every step of the journey to success for AMC from the ground up.

Faculty, trustees, administration, and students made presentations on the implications of Ex Corde Ecclesiae for Anna Maria College.

XV

THE EARLY NINETIES

As faculty and administrators prepared the golden jubilee of the college in 1996, they reviewed the mission of the college and became even more aware of the benchmarks by which they and the college would be judged: quality, relevance, service, and fiscal viability. They looked for levers of change such as content of programs, course delivery, and new skills needed by students and faculty. They also questioned what values needed to be emphasized within the campus community—not only pragmatic values, but especially values of the heart and mind.

On all fronts activity prevailed. Buildings of an earlier vintage needed modernization and renovation. The institutional blueprint, based on the long- range plans for 1988-92,[83] brought into focus a number of needs: such as, the creation of a performing arts center to be carved out of the large auditorium in Foundress Hall, contemporization of the chapel built in 1963, and the updating of designs and styles in many other areas. As a result, fund-raising efforts increased in several creative ways. The participation of the alumni was gratifying. Phone-a-thons were their most rewarding fund-raising tool. Faculty, staff, alumni, and students took turns in reaching alumni across the country. The capital funds campaigns, undertaken to build the library and the activities center, had vastly increased the donor base. AMC had a wide network of friends and supporters. Undeniably, in development, nothing simply happens; someone makes it happen. Planning was necessary, coordination was critical, but action was all important. All of these elements were in place at this crucial time in the physical growth of AMC.

In 1990, again in accordance with the long-range plan for 1988-92, the college met its goal by raising more than one million dollars to complete the renovation of the chapel and create a performing arts center. Major benefactors contributed greatly to the attainment of that goal. Other donors responded to the appeal for chapel

Re-dedication of the chapel by Bishop Bernard J. Flanagan, May 5, 1990.

opportunity to strengthen the ties binding them to their Alma Mater. More important, it was a rare occasion to exchange notes with friends and favorite teachers. The event became a sharing of values by which the alumni lived and made decisions. Everyone benefitted. In the presence of loved ones, values that usually are deep in the heart rose to the surface, and an exchange became a revitalization for the persons involved.

On May 5,[84] the chapel, built in 1963, was re-dedicated. It was a glorious event which will remain etched in the minds and hearts of all the participants for years to come. The hope was that this renovation would add a striking new dimension to the spiritual journey of the campus faith community and thus favor the fulfillment of the college mission to foster religious sensitivity. This rare occasion promoted those values of the heart and mind which need new vigor to be enlivened and productive. The chapel featured original stained

windows and the more substantial pieces; such as, the altar, the baptismal font, and the ambo. Although the chapel and the performing arts center were campaign priorities, there were sufficient funds to equip a biotechnology laboratory, update a computer science center, modernize classroom furniture, renovate several conference rooms, and undertake campus beautification.

Spring 1990 was marked by a number of events which will go down in history. On April 7, a special gourmet dinner welcomed the classes who left Anna Maria College forty, thirty-five, thirty, and twenty-five years before. The evening was full of festivity, laughter, and warmth. The anniversary classes looked forward to this annual event at which they were guests of the president. It was an

A front view of the renovated chapel. Note the original stained glass windows.

glass windows, a baptismal font, and an imposing oak altar. Bishop Bernard J. Flanagan re-dedicated the chapel, assisted by the college chaplain, Father Conrad Pecevich, and eight other members of the clergy.

On May 12,[85] at 12 noon, the dedication of the Zecco Performing Arts Center was held. Created from the thirty-three-year-old auditorium, it provided permanent seating for 350 people with the possibility of some additional 100 seats in adjacent rooms separated from the Center by movable walls. The Center was a state-of-the-art facility. It was called the Zecco Performing Arts Center to honor the parents of the major donors, Patrick and Janice Zecco. The plaque in the lobby of the Center reads as follows:

In grateful appreciation
to our parents
Patrick G. & Dorothy Zecco
and
Russell & Joyce Betteridge
in whose honor this center
is dedicated
May 12, 1990
Patrick and Janice Zecco

The same day, May 12 at 4:00 P.M., the reredos window in the renovated chapel was unveiled in a very original manner. With lights on only at both entrances of the chapel, the family of Dr. Lucille Ouellette, class of '68, trustee of AMC, and donor of the reredos, assembled in the center seats along with members of the campus community. The college chaplain blessed the window which was then illuminated to reveal a beautiful stained glass rendering of the rising sun. It was a wonderful sight! A few minutes later, all the lights were turned on and Mass was celebrated. Following the Eucharist, the Ouellette family and their guests enjoyed a special dinner in their honor. At 6:00 P.M., after the festive dinner, they and other guests met at St. Joseph's Hall (the science building) where the

biotechnology laboratory was formally dedicated to honor Dr. Ouellette, whose expertise and generosity made it possible. The guests heard a brief account of the use of this laboratory room, and the event ended with a reception in the lower level of the building.

The following day, Sunday, May 13, a plaque commemorating the gift of the altar by the Caparso family, in honor of their mother, was unveiled before the 10:30 A.M. Mass. The plaque reads as follows:

This altar given
to Anna Maria College
in honor of Mary R. Caparso
by her children as
an expression of their love
and acknowledgement
of her significance
in each of their lives.
Mother's Day, May 13, 1990

Bishop George E. Rueger and Reverend Francis Kelly, both trustees, were on hand to celebrate this Mother's Day Mass.

On May 16, a full awards program began with attendance at Mass at 6:30 P.M. in the newly renovated chapel. After Mass, members of the campus community assembled in the sparkling new Zecco Center where the major event of the evening took place. *A Good Teacher Award* of $1,000 from the Sears Foundation went to Sister Clarice Chauvin who was the choice of the award committee composed of administrators, faculty, alumni, and students. To follow the teaching career of Sister Clarice is to study the lifetime of a dedicated, intelligent, and highly resourceful individual. The second number of the program was a special faculty recognition for three members of the faculty for their recent publications: Dr. Thomas Del Prete, Dr. Ramiro Ramirez, and Dr. Paul Russell. In addition, Dr. Robert Goepfert was recognized for his unswerving dedication to the continued publication of *Spectrum*, a multi-disciplinary publica-

GRADUATION 1991

The spring of 1991 was one of the most glorious I can remember in New England. In April, temperatures were in the 60s and by May, it was already in the 70s. We had no rain in May, just bright sunshine, so much so that students spent as much time outside tanning as they did in the library studying for their exams! The forecast for Saturday, May 25, Graduation Day, was for a potential thunderstorm.

For the first time, Caparso Field, because of the beauty of its location, had been selected as the site for graduation exercises. Never had so much time been spent on manicuring the lawn and seeing to every detail. There would be no tent to hide any of its beauty! As I drove to the campus, the sky in the west looked ominous, so threatening that I grabbed a small umbrella to conceal beneath my robes. I saw that Caparso Field had been set up with a stage for the dignitaries and an ocean of chairs for students and faculty. However, there was no protection for a potential shower.

Attorney John J. Curtin receives his honorary degree from Sister Bernadette Madore, president, in the library after fleeing torrential rain on the graduation field.

By the time we robed and marched toward Miriam Hall, I felt a couple of droplets, but nothing significant. A brass band with musicians in tuxedos played Elgar's "Pomp and Circumstance" while we took our seats and dignitaries assumed their place on the stage. Just as the band was finishing the National Anthem, suddenly the sky opened with a torrential downpour. I pushed the button to open my umbrella. Dean Ann-Marie McMorrow Hepburn announced from the stage that we would forego the speeches and present the undergraduate degrees, hoping that the downpour would be brief.

Suddenly, a great bolt of chain lightning struck the western horizon and the torrent increased. I saw professor Parente bolt in a run toward Foundress Hall. Professor Janet Fisher and I followed at a fast clip. By the time we reached the shelter of the lobby of Foundress Hall, we observed a stampede of faculty, students, administrators, and trustees; all were completely drenched. Graduation robes began to run in multicolored rivers down legs and arms. More elaborate hair styles collapsed as applied cosmetics dissolved into tiny brooks, adding tributaries to our stress of disappointment.

While the Registrar attempted to hand out degrees from her office to a swarm of dripping candidates, the recipients of honorary degrees were offered tributes in the library. At Vice President Charles Hepburn's feet was a large puddle of water. His magnificent Stanford University doctoral robes were ruined. Undaunted by this, he gave praise and thanks for the careers of deserving people, who were not quite prepared for an "underwater graduation." If commencement 1991 was to be the most spectacular since 1950—it was indeed—but in unexpected ways!

— Paul A. Russell, Ph.D.,
Chairperson of the history/political science department

tion produced on campus and circulated throughout the academic community across the country. Others recognized were Richard L. Connors and Paul D. Hand for their twenty-five years of service to Anna Maria College. The entire program was dedicated to Father Conrad Pecevich, chaplain, who left AMC to pursue his doctorate in ministry.

In 1991, Anna Maria College celebrated its 45th anniversary with a mardi-gras fund-raising dinner dance in Mechanics Hall; a faculty/administrator/staff/student reception; and, for the Sisters of Saint Anne, a special celebration including a gala luncheon and Mass of thanksgiving. This was an opportunity for the campus community to rejoice in one another's accomplishments over the years, to meet and be more acutely aware of the support and interest of many friends from the larger community, and to review Anna Maria College's journey through its history. Minds and hearts were filled with joy in the present and hope for the future.

In the summer of 1992, in keeping with the college long-range plans, much work was done to upgrade Madonna Hall, the main entrance to Trinity Hall, the portico of St. Joseph Hall, and the entire snack bar area. Roofs at Socquet House, Esther House, Miriam Hall, Cardinal Cushing Hall, and Campus Center received new, full or partial coverings. Work was also done on the new baseball and softball playing fields. The for-

Sister Bernadette Madore's interest in the campus knew no bounds. Here, she climbed into a cherry picker to get a better view of things.

mer formal lounge was renovated and became the *Jacques Conference Room*, dedicated to the memory of Gertrude Bolduc Jacques, mother of Elise A. Jacques, M.D., class of '69, and generous benefactor. The *Helfenbein Room* and the *Nolder Room*, conference rooms adjacent to the main hall in the Zecco Center, were also dedicated in special ceremonies to honor other benefactors of the college; namely, Gerald and Marilyn Helfenbein, and Barbara Nolder, class of '65. Elise Jacques, Gerald Helfenbein, and Barbara Nolder were also members of the board of trustees.

The former studio in Miriam Hall was totally transformed and rebuilt in the summer of 1992. The two-story room, in its contemporized appearance, was named the *Payer Room* in honor of Sister M. Madeleine of the Savior (Jeannette Payer), first chairperson of the music department. With a capacity for eighty persons, it featured acoustical ceiling "clouds," a stage with an acoustical shell, a parquet floor, and special lighting. It was destined primarily for music activities, faculty and guest recitals, providing the audience with an intimate concert hall experience. The renovation was made possible by alumna Rosalie Rocheleau Grenon and her husband, David, whose challenge gift was matched by other alumni and friends of the college. New acquisitions, repairs, and refurbishing added substantially to the attractive appearance of the building. Music and art were among the first fields of concentration offered by AMC in

President Madore presents key to the Jacques Room *to Elise A. Jacques, M.D.*

President Madore presents key to the Helfenbein Room *to Gerald Helfenbein.*

imitation of Mother Marie Anne who, in the very early days of the congregation, favored the teaching of music and art in her little country school of Vaudreuil.

At Anna Maria College, drama was also supported. In the early decades, a dramatic club under the direction of Sister M. John of Carmel

President Madore presents key to the Nolder Room *to Barbara Nolder.*

(Clarice Chauvin) staged plays by Aeschylus, Shakespeare, Miller, Wilder, Hansberry, Hellman, and others. To acquaint students with the foundress of the Sisters of Saint Anne, Louise Cristina, class of 1960, composed and recited a poem to the background music of Vivaldi's "The Four Seasons" which was then pantomimed and later presented along with a slide show on separate occasions of Foundress Day which was always celebrated close to April 18, birthday of the foundress. This special event recalled the foundress whose congregation made AMC possible. It was a gala day, celebrated for over thirty years, when students and faculty gathered for a special meal and enjoyed presentations of drama, dance, and music appropriate for the occasion.

In 1990, to further promote drama at AMC the construction of the Zecco performing arts center was undertaken. This enterprise involved a substantial risk. Unless properly managed, used, and promoted, the center could become an albatross instead of an opportunity to present art in many of its more delightful forms. In 1992, the success of the production by Virginia Byrnes of Robert Bolt's "A Man for All Seasons" prompted Tom Saupe, manager of the Zecco performing arts center, to approach the administration of the college with the idea of supporting the New England Theatre Company as a group in residence at the college. As part of its commitment to the arts and public outreach, Anna Maria embraced the idea and never regretted it. Thereafter, the New England Theatre Company (NETC) utilized the Zecco performing arts center on campus as a home theater performing full seasons of productions including classical and contemporary plays and musicals. At the college, NETC worked with students, faculty, and staff either in the classroom or on stage for special projects including workshops in theatrical subjects open to students and the public at large. NETC has enjoyed continued highly laudatory critical reviews and has been referred to as "the thinking person's community theater group."[86]

In 1990, the Sisters of Saint Anne celebrated the hundredth anniversary of the death of their foundress, Esther Blondin, known as Mother Marie Anne. To raise awareness among Anna Maria College students of Mother Marie Anne's importance in the founding of the college, the president made available three scholarships for students who succeeded in a directed research on the life of Esther Blondin and her influence at all levels of education.

To assist Catholic colleges and universities in determining whether they are truly Catholic, Pope John Paul II, in 1990, issued a set of general guidelines in the document *Ex Corde Ecclesiae.*[87] It was widely discussed in the Catholic academic world, and on September 14, 1991, at a convocation held on campus, Sister Alice Gallin, O.S.U., discussed the meaning of a Catholic college. Faculty, trustees, administrators, and students made presentations on the implications of *Ex Corde Ecclesiae* for Anna Maria College. A correlation between the vision and mission of the college and the papal document clarified the responsibilities of the college community. Four committees met throughout the following year to discuss mission and identity, academics, governance, and student life—an in-depth study of the college vision in light of *Ex Corde Ecclesiae.*[88]

Reports of the discussions held by these four committees were heard at the October Planning Day and the January Faculty Days. Further discussion followed. Dr. Walter Noyalis,[89] chairman of the department of religious studies, circulated a report to be used as a guide for ongoing study of the document. The perennial questions, relative to the degree to which the college was considered Catholic, were on the table and the answers bore the stamp of the present time and cultural context in which the college existed. Every time such questions were posed the RSQ (religious and spiritual quotient) of the campus community rose. However, to remain at the high level desired necessitated much spiritual energy. It is a lasting and serious duty of members of the campus ministry staff to lead faculty and stu-

---

WHY ANNA MARIA COLLEGE?

*I*f I had to do it all over again I would still go to AMC. I loved the social life of the dorm, the family-like learning environment of the music department, my friends and my teachers, the professors. The experience helped me to grow into the person I am today. It wasn't until September of freshman year that I started to figure out who I really was. It was the first time I was totally away from anything that was familiar to me and I was away from my family in a new situation with new friends. I cannot name all the people that have touched my life and made a difference. There are too many. The opportunities for me at AMC were limitless: student government, V-shows, tennis, recitals, etc. I once found a saying that seemed to sum up my time at AMC: "You never really leave a place you love—part of it you take with you leaving a part of you behind."

— *Heidi Johnston Richard, Class of 1991*

dents in the search for practical answers.

Service, a benchmark established by the college mission, found expression in the establishment of the Center for Professional Studies[90] in the fall of 1992. The center was designed to place a college degree in business, criminal justice, nursing, and paralegal studies within the reach of older students—part-time students who needed schedules suited to their family and employment responsibilities. All courses were offered during late afternoons, evenings, or Saturdays. This center was a response to the demands of the community at large and those of the market place for academic service to older adults involved in career changes leading to upward professional mobility. Under the direction of Assistant Dean Joanne Charette, the center grew dramatically and in 1995-1996 the large number of students who enrolled accounted for a doubling of tuition income over the previous year.

As in the seventies and later in the eighties,

Thumbs up at Graduation 1990.

Sr. Clarice Chauvin carrying the mace and leading the graduation processional, 1990.

experimentation with new programs continued to determine relevance or lack of sufficient interest. When the latter was clear, the college abandoned the program and studied market demands to reach a more exact level of response. An example of such a program was Fire Science, designed for individuals holding an associate degree in Fire Science and employed or seeking employment in fields related to fire prevention and fire protection. This unique program allowed adults to pursue advanced professional development and education on a part-time basis through the Center for Professional Studies. The program was highly relevant and met with success. Relevance, as a benchmark, was highlighted once again when, for the first time, three Anna Maria College students were accepted into the Washington, D.C. Internship Program in the fall of 1991.[91] The program was and continues to be highly competitive. The three participants agreed that the experience was pertinent to their search for career direction; it heightened awareness of politics and enlarged the boundaries of their academic disciplines. They claimed that the experience could not be replicated in a classroom.

Quality and viability, as benchmarks, gained prominence at the end of fiscal year 1992 when all the components of the long-range plan were reviewed and evaluated against best practice. Each plan received one of the following ratings: accomplished, deferred, ongoing, or abandoned.

The academic year 1991-92 heralded several rapid changes in the leadership of the college. In June 1991, Sister Bernadette Madore, president of Anna Maria College since 1977, announced her retirement, effective June 30, 1992. A search committee for the choice of a new president was assembled. Major philosophical differences fractured the committee and brought about its dissolution. The incoming chairperson of the board of trustees, Sister Jeannette Robichaud, S.S.A., asked President Madore to extend her tenure and she retired one year later than anticipated, on June 30, 1993. The board of trustees appointed Sister Bernadette Madore, upon her retirement, to the position of chancellor to maintain the presence of a Sister of Saint Anne on an administrative level. Less than two years later, under Dr. Dill, the title was abolished and Sister Bernadette was honored as president *emerita*. Her successor as president was Sister Rita Larivee, S.S.A., who served as the fifth president of AMC until December 31, 1994, when she returned to Loyola University in Chicago to complete her doctoral studies. Dr. William R. Dill became interim president and served until June 30, 1996,[92] when Dr. Bernard S. Parker was appointed seventh president of Anna Maria College.[93]

In 1992, Kenneth F. Black was appointed vice president for business affairs and treasurer, and the business office was streamlined. A new budget-reporting format, making monthly reviews clearer, faster, and simpler, was adopted. It eliminated interface obstacles with other offices; elaborated a flexible formula predicated on actual student enrollment for the granting of

financial aid; accelerated tuition payments through an agency supplying consolidated payments for banks dealing with student loans; and used electronic funds transfer (EFT) to obtain instant payment of loans of all kinds.

After a period of negotiations by the treasurer, Ken Black, Paxton Electric Company reduced fees to the college by $40,000 to $45,000; Paxton Water Department issued a rate reduction of $6,000; and negotiations with Honeywell, Inc., paved the way for the modernization of certain facilities, maintenance of equipment and systems, improved operating efficiency, and reduction of operating costs, and College Bookstores of America took over bookstore operations.[94]

On January 4, 1993, the on-campus security force changed from a contracted service company to a more cost-effective in-house security system providing 24-hour vigilance. Paul M. Chenevert, former deputy superintendent in charge of operations with the Middlesex County Sheriff's Department, became the new chief of security. Immediately, he enhanced the reputation of AMC as a safe campus. Under the new system, the residence was locked 24 hours a day with magnetic cards providing entry. All residence rooms were re-keyed. In addition to twelve officers, five student interns provided escort and parking service, campus patrol, and building checks.

On February 1, 1994, Paxton Police Chief Robert J. Mortell was shot to death in a small wooded area in Holden, close to the Paxton line. To maintain the legacy of Chief Mortell, a distinguished alumnus, the Mortell Institute was founded on the AMC campus to provide a forum to examine public policy and effect change through exchange of ideas, promotion of cooperative efforts, and training and education of public safety practitioners. The mission and purpose of the Institute admirably supported the college mission in providing an opportunity to foster, especially in law-enforcing officers, intellectual involvement, social awareness, and dedication to justice and peace. The first program under the auspices of the Mortell Institute featured a presentation by Dr. Edwin J. Delattre of Boston University who stressed the need for integrity in the law enforcement officer. The following words by Dr. DeLattre are worthy of note:

Good sheriffs and other law enforcement leaders have always understood that integrity is not negotiable....The purpose of...training is to produce strong and brave men. Not men of physical courage alone, but men of great moral courage who can

IN MEMORIAM

Ann-Marie L. McMorrow Hepburn, undergraduate academic dean since 1988 died on May 31, 1993 in the Medical Center of Central Massachusetts. Before serving as dean, Ann-Marie was chairperson of the department of biology where she also served as a faculty member. "Annie"as she was affectionately called was with Anna Maria College all of her professional life, which extended over thirty years. In addition, she was an undergraduate student at AMC for four years and befriended students and colleagues alike. No one will ever know how many people she touched—how many she helped. We remember her with deep affection.

In March 1993, Mary Plunkett died at the age of ninety-six. For 18 years Mrs. Plunkett was supervisor of practice teachers at Anna Maria College. She served on the faculty and taught in both the sociology and education departments. During her career at AMC, Mrs. Plunkett served as coordinator of financial aid and as the first supervisor of social work placement. She retired in 1972 and, in 1973, she received an honorary doctorate in education from the college in recognition of her many years of service to Anna Maria College and its students.

— Report of the President 1992-1993, p. 11

Mary Plunkett

Ann-Marie McMorrow

face unflinchingly the hoots and jeers of weaker men who secretly respect and envy them....The ability and desire to resist temptation, to fight against the easy way is the test of the man....It takes great moral stamina to make the right decision which generally is unpopular....

These many examples of growth, physical and otherwise, described in this chapter provided an opportunity for the entire campus community and the alumni to resonate the values of relevance and generosity. These values inspired in many donors the largesse to make the dreams of others come true.

As the decade of the nineties took its first steps on the path of time and placed historical stakes along the way, technology leaped powerfully down that path and broadened it into a superhighway. In effect, its applications created a paradigm shift—a new version of reality. While the reality of the world of higher education was changing, technology provided a resource to accommodate the rate of change occurring. Life without technology was hardly an option, as the reader will discover in the next chapter.

Some Faculty and Staff
Known to Generations of Students.

Sr. Therese Dion

Dr. Edward Cole

Duane Quinn

Fr. Henry Donoghue

Dr. Lorraine Popowicz

Sr. Colombe Theoret

Kathryn Boudreau

Carol Williams

Sr. Donalda

Ralph Parente

Gerald Garrity

Frances Delaney

Sr. Elaine Caron

Sr. Lorraine Marie

Cynthia Taylor

Sr. Lorraine Bilodeau

Sr. Rita Carrier

Meg Kirkendall

Maureen Egan

Dr. Jeanne Tasse

Pauline Snell

Christine Kisiel

Dr. Ramiro Ramirez

Mary Ann Foley

Roger Greene

Fr. Roland Hebert

Dr. William Gannon

Jayne Witt

Dr. Stuart Block

Sr. M. Louis Arthur Moll

Sr. Barbara Flynn

Sr. Jeannette Robichaud

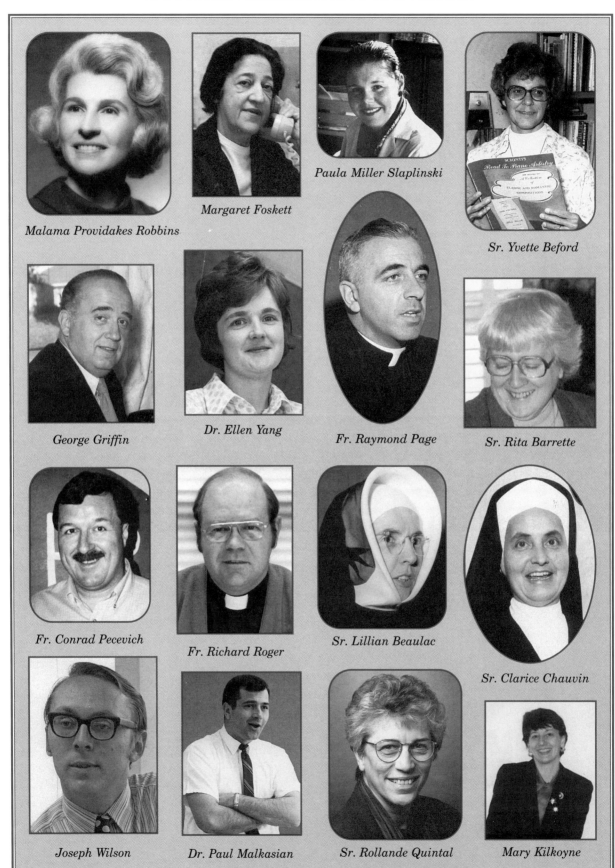

Malama Providakes Robbins

Margaret Foskett

Paula Miller Slaplinski

Sr. Yvette Beford

George Griffin

Dr. Ellen Yang

Fr. Raymond Page

Sr. Rita Barrette

Fr. Conrad Pecevich

Fr. Richard Roger

Sr. Lillian Beaulac

Sr. Clarice Chauvin

Joseph Wilson

Dr. Paul Malkasian

Sr. Rollande Quintal

Mary Kilkoyne

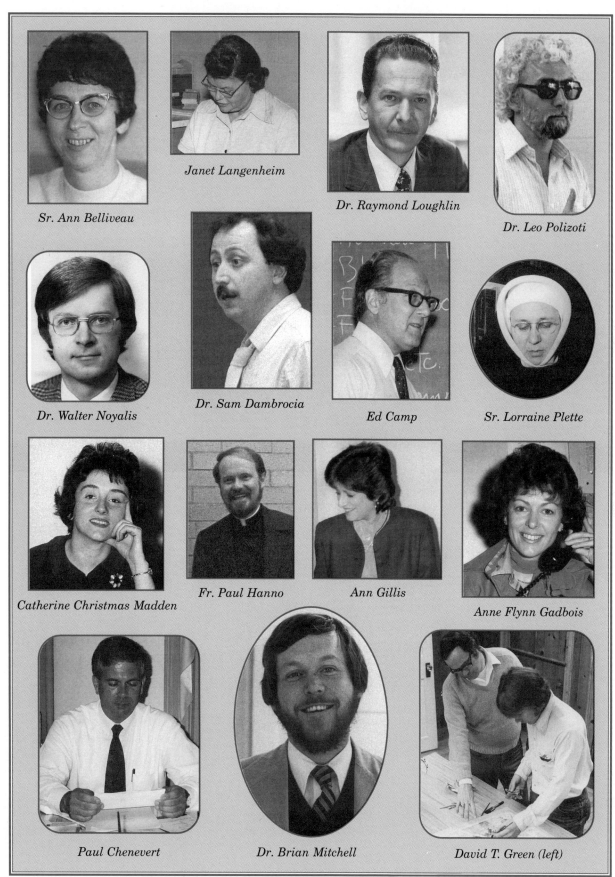

Sr. Ann Belliveau

Janet Langenheim

Dr. Raymond Loughlin

Dr. Leo Polizoti

Dr. Walter Noyalis

Dr. Sam Dambrocia

Ed Camp

Sr. Lorraine Plette

Catherine Christmas Madden

Fr. Paul Hanno

Ann Gillis

Anne Flynn Gadbois

Paul Chenevert

Dr. Brian Mitchell

David T. Green (left)

*As the college came to the threshold
of its fifty-year existence, it could be
proud of its ability to remain sensitive
to the needs of the time.*

XVI

A PARADIGM SHIFT

*I*n the nineties, there was an urgency for change across the academic world. It was essential that the powers of technology be used to enhance learning at every level. Post-secondary education benchmarking was a moving target and it was clear that " business as usual" was out. All colleges and universities, including Anna Maria, were caught in a web of compliance, market, and external forces that required substantive re-engineering from informed leaders, and technology was recognized as one of the world's engines of change. The eighties had witnessed a rising interest in the information superhighway, and Anna Maria College dealt actively with the paradigm shift which technology promoted. Sister Rita Larivee, a computer expert, tapped the efficiencies of technology and dispelled the fears of those who looked askance at it.

During the years 1993 to 1996, under Presidents Rita Larivee, S.S.A. and William R. Dill efforts were made to complete wiring the campus and make technology a vital working force. The ultimate vision for the distant future was an environment of integrated technologies hosting state-of-the-art multimedia teaching conditions, both on campus and in a distance learning format.

A good technology program is one featuring a total network which is as inclusive, reliable, and effective as state-of-the-art telephones. It requires an involved, well-equipped, and knowledgeable faculty, higher education's most important asset. For the faculty, information technology provided new leverage. It was expected that students would gradually have their own computers and be able to plug them in for exercises around the campus, and that faculty would move from a lecture-teaching approach to one of guiding and coaching active learning among their students.

In the summer of 1994, Anna Maria College entered into an alliance with IBM—a partner with strong overall skills. In addition to its cabling skills for the design and implementation of the physical network, IBM was uniquely qual-

169

ified in the design, implementation, start-up, and trouble-shooting phases of AMC's pilot project necessary to insure a successful completion.

Anna Maria College, during that summer (1994), moved forward on the installation and implementation of the physical network infrastructure and the completion of the campus-wide fiber optic backbone. The planning that preceded installation provided for a structural backbone that not only served present needs, but also anticipated, well into the next century, all future expansion and advanced technology when these became available.

Significantly, Sister Rita Larivee had already installed, during the previous years, a "starter network" which had achieved the desired effect of building demand for network connections and services among faculty and staff.

The project engineered by Sister Rita Larivee with IBM met with great success and provided the substance for the development of a 2 to 1 matching grant proposal of $300,000 to the Alden Trust. The request for a matching grant

was successful. Consequently, during the tenure of Sister Rita's successor, Dr. Dill, matching funds were raised and used—making it possible for the treasurer, Ken Black, to carry out further negotiations with IBM to bring to completion the campus technological infrastructure. It would be a critical resource as applications continued to be distributed, distance learning became prevalent, and national education delivery systems evolved.

All buildings, whether administrative, operational, residential, or educational, were connected to one of three local area networks through fiber optic cable. Cable television and voice and data connections for all student rooms were provided in the residence. Furthermore, students and employees were granted electronic mail accounts which allowed them to establish electronic communication throughout the world. Each residence room had a direct network connection and students could access with ease e-mail and the internet through their personal computers.[95] For students who did not own a

---

MARKET-DRIVEN PARADIGM SHIFTS

*F*rom August of 1992 through August of 1996, Anna Maria College experienced substantive swings in its enrollment, financial capacity, infrastructure, and teaching/learning technology access. Early in the period, demographic realities imposed operating losses and current fund deficits that galvanized the college's leadership and the directors of graduate and other continuing education programs to meet the challenge. Revenue side management was given the highest priority and value-add criteria were applied to new cost elements. It took the first year to reverse the negative financial trend and for the entire campus community to initiate what was to become an exciting mastery of market-driven paradigm shifts.

The college became increasingly aware of its external presence and opportunities in the form of consortium collaboration, strategic business alliances, cost sharing, and technology utilization. Imagination, negotiation, searches for grants, new continuing education revenue flows, and development all combined to resource and enable change management. The construction of a new technology infrastructure networked the campus and brought global linkages to faculty and students. One memorable application comes to mind when a world-wide web site inquiry plotted a road map to attend the AMC basketball team's first appearance in the division III NCAA sweet sixteen tournament.

— *Kenneth F. Black, Chief Financial Officer, 1992-1996*

TECHNOLOGY AT ANNA MARIA COLLEGE

*T*oday, a liberal arts education includes the ability to use information and technology effectively. Anna Maria College recognized this reality in the early eighties and has since continued to integrate it across the campus. Within a span of fifteen years, the college went from two stand-alone Apple II computers located in the library (and acquired through Title III funds) to a complete technological infrastructure designed with state-of-the-art equipment.

The administration, with great foresight, elicited, encouraged, and supported the interest of the faculty and thus allowed much more to be accomplished than would have seemed possible. The college's distinctive ability to rally around a goal made possible timely responses to the demands for technological know-how.

Technology is not always easy to use; it requires deep interest, risk-taking, and willingness to forage in unknown territory. For those of us who have played a role in kick-starting the program, the fruits of our labor are self-evident. Anna Maria College has truly evolved into a liberal arts college for the twenty-first century.

— *Rita Larivee, S.S.A., PhD., President of AMC, 1993-1994*

computer, there were small computer labs, open 24 hours a day, in the residences in addition to two other computer labs in other buildings open through hours of operation. PCs, servers, printers, and LAN-based software were purchased. Elzbieta Sobocinski, coordinator of computer information services, and her assistants: Patti Keller, Patrick McEvoy, and Joe Kane were everywhere! Training was provided for end users in the areas of PC basics, network access/usage, and software packages. In 1996, laptops were available to faculty to enable them to move from their campus offices to their homes without loss of continuity.

The digital culture was already making its mark on the changing landscape of higher education, and the wired information infrastructure enabled faculty to capture the spirit of change, innovation, and opportunity heralded by the new wired world. They looked for practical means to turn the electronic revolution into a successful tool for teaching and learning at Anna Maria College. Furthermore, they realized that it

was critical to have widespread collaboration and cooperation among faculty and academic support staff to facilitate planning, decision-making, and assistance for faculty and students. Hence,

IMPACT OF TECHNOLOGY

*O*ne of the changes having the greatest impact on career services has been the incorporation of computer technology to the department. The career center disseminates information not only to on-campus students, but also to commuters, evening students, alumni, and satellite sites through its home page. The home page includes a Job Opportunity Bulletin, (listing all professional jobs) as well as links to Job Trak (a national job listing service) and the Massachusetts Educational Recruiting Consortium (job listing for teachers). Students are updated on career fairs and events and provided with graduate school information, as well as general career-related advice.

— *Judith Sparanges, Director, Career Services*

Anna Maria College developed an on-campus *Teaching, Learning, and Technology Roundtable* connected to the American Association for Higher Education TLTR program. The TLTR on the AMC campus was composed of top administrators, faculty, administrative staff, and students. The membership was broken down into sub-committees where the critical and ongoing work was done. The aim was to fulfill the desires of administrators and faculty who wanted students to have greater access to digital opportunities, to participate more fully in professional conversations, to collaborate more easily with peers, to ask questions and exchange ideas more frequently and comfortably with faculty members, to learn more on their own, and generally to have more power in the teaching-learning equation.

Needless to say, conceptual and problem-solving skills were tested to the highest level and AMC's "wired" campus soon became the envy of other small colleges. This effort, on the part of the college, was a clear expression of the mission which was to provide quality education by fostering intellectual involvement and career preparation. The value added was also an excellent response to market demands.

While lending her support and expertise to the wiring of the college and the completion of its network infrastructure, Sister Rita turned her attention to other important matters relative to academic and financial advancement, recruitment and enrollment of students and the renovation of buildings in need of modernization.

To strengthen the academic identity of Anna Maria College in its offering of professional programs in a liberal arts context and to solidify the college's niche among colleges, Sister Rita promoted the development of the Universal Curriculum, a concept intended to blend and integrate professional programs within the liberal arts core. Faculty and students responded to her efforts and enthusiasm, and there was greater understanding and harmony among the proponents of professional programs and the supporters of "pure" liberal arts. Furthermore, to attract well-prepared and successful high school seniors, the president established what was termed: the Presidential Scholars Programs. Those programs were highly successful in raising the intellectual quotient of incoming classes. Working with Ken Black, the vice president for financial affairs, President Larivee encouraged the identification of new revenue streams and the search for grant monies. She kept the bottom line out of the red and the budget in a healthy position. In addition, Sister Rita undertook the renovation of the Moll Art Center and created a beautifully designed exhibition hall called St. Luke's Gallery. This hall was used to showcase the major exhibits of the jubilee year.

Sensitive to the needs of the non-athlete students Sister Rita promoted the construction of a small but very adequate outdoor recreation area, in proximity to the residence.

The urgency for change mentioned earlier was felt and responded to by the leaders of the institution. President Larivee and later President Dill realized that normalcy was yesterday's reality and the paradigm shift taking place required new reality. As the college came to the threshold of its fifty-year existence, it could be proud of its ability to remain sensitive to the needs of the time. Much value had been added since its foundation. In celebrating its fifty years of service, it turned the spotlight on women and men who had used their energies, talents, and skills to further the mission of Anna Maria College.

The Changing Face of Socquet House

Top: Socquet House in 1895 when it was the home of David Harrington. The stable to the right is where Trinity Hall now stands. Bottom: Socquet house, pictured here in the eighties, was the administrative hub of the college from 1980-1997.

Socquet House in 1952.

On June 1, 1952, *The Catholic Free Press* announced the transfer of Anna Maria College to the Worcester diocese. The farmhouse on "Mooreacres," the 293-acre country estate on Sunset Lane in Paxton, became the residence of the Sisters of Saint Anne who staffed the college.

Aerial view of Socquet House in 1980. Note the dog house to the left under the trees.

*U*ntil 1967, Socquet House was the residence of the Sisters. From 1967 to 1980, it housed the Moll Art Center, and from 1980 to 1997, it served as the administrative center of the college. In 1997, it became once again the residence of the Sisters of St. Anne.

Below: Dedication of Socquet House on September 26, 1980. (Left to right) William V. Guerin, chairman of the board of trustees, Sr. Irene Socquet, and Bishop Bernard J. Flanagan.

"We want to be known, as we are by many of our graduates, as a school which gives excellent value for the money invested."

— President William Dill

XVII

ANNA MARIA COLLEGE CELEBRATES ITS 50TH BIRTHDAY

To mark the golden anniversary year of Anna Maria College, and fifty years of dedication to high-quality affordable education, Dr. William R. Dill, interim president, announced that there would be no increase in tuition or room and board charges for full-time undergraduate students enrolling for the 1996-1997 year. The charges remained at $11,230 for tuition and $5,028 for room and board. Dr. Dill reflected as follows:

Over the years we have worked hard to keep our prices at reasonable levels and, with financial aid, to help as many families as we can to meet these costs. We want to be known, as we are by many of our graduates, as a school which gives excellent value for the money invested—in program options, in good teaching, in individual attention and support, and in opportunities through classes, sports, internships, and other activities for personal growth....

Dr. William R. Dill, President of AMC, 1995-1996.

The college will keep operating with an eye to making this an ever better place for a great undergraduate experience. Last year, we made a large number of state-of-the-art, multimedia computers available to students in the library, the learning center, and the residence hall. This year [1996] we have expanded e-mail and CD-Rom usage, opened access to internet, and helped faculty learn how to assist students in taking advantage of the new learning resources. We have finished wiring classrooms, offices, and all the residence hall rooms so that all are computer and cable network ready....

Dr. Dill continued in this vein:

Happily, many of the improvements we are making do not involve more money. They come from spirit and dedication, such as the great competitive success of this year's [1996] Division III men's and women's basket ball teams; and the wonderful period of service that Anna Maria nursing students and graduates performed during winter break at hospitals in Lithuania....[96]

Another reason to celebrate was the ranking AMC received from *Money Guide*, published annually by *Money Magazine*.[97] The 1996 edition ranked Anna Maria College eighteenth among the top twenty-five schools nationally that combine high academic quality with a "premium on religion in their curriculum or campus life." AMC was one of only three New England colleges among the twenty-five that made the

The Sisters of St. Anne in residence at AMC, 1995.
Seated left to right: Sr. Irene Socquet, Sr. Clarence Marie, Sr. Bernadette Madore.
Standing left to right: Sr. Lorraine Bilodeau, Sr. Lorraine Plette, Sr. Christine,
Sr. Clarice Chauvin, Sr. Lillian Beaulac, Sr. Pauline Madore.

list. College selection was based on 16 educational factors: entrance examination results, class rank, high school grade point average, faculty resources, core faculty, faculty deployment, library resources, instructional budget, student services budget, freshman retention rate, four-year graduation rates, advanced study, default ratio on student loans, graduates who earn doctorates, and business success. In addition, the AMC Graduate Division ranked number 20 among the 25 largest graduate schools in Massachusetts surpassing Worcester Polytechnic Institute, Western New England College, Brandeis University, and Massachusetts School of Law.

President Dill, Mary Kilcoyne, director of institutional advancement, and the 50th anniversary committee met weekly in preparation for the Golden Year of 1996. Special anniversary letterhead and envelopes with embossed foil were available. The anniversary kick-off was Wednesday, January 24 at 4:00 P.M. President Dill and the entire college community met in the dining hall for cake, punch, and special memories, presented by some of our alumni: Suzanne Kelly, '59; Christine Kardokas, '65; Paula Conrad, '69; Kevin Mayne, '81; Mark

> ## THE SISTERS OF SAINT ANNE AFTER 50 YEARS
>
> *D*espite all of the changes that have occurred over the past fifty years, the Sisters of Saint Anne are still very much part of this campus. First and foremost, they are still our sponsors, and they are assuming their leadership role on the college's board of trustees. And while they are no longer the visible presence they once were, they continue—very quietly—to pray and work for our personal and institutional betterment.
>
> *— Robert J. Lemieux,*
> *Professor of philosophy and French*

Georgeson, '86; and Brian Richard, '92. The second scheduled event was St. Patrick's Day Alumni Breakfast at O'Connors Restaurant & Pub, made more Irish than ever for the occasion! The guest speaker was Kevin O'Sullivan, director of marketing for the Worcester Area Chamber of Commerce. A number of other celebratory events followed suit through the spring of 1996. On March 28, 1996, at the Gates Lane School of International Studies, the Anna Maria College alumni council sponsored a fiftieth anniversary party to celebrate the service to education of AMC's Worcester teachers. Large numbers assembled at 3:30 for the festivities.

> ## TRADITION
>
> *W*hen I as a young sister of Saint Anne working on a B.A. degree, I witnessed the construction of several campus buildings. Over the years, I saw two or three editions of various campus services: chapel, library, classrooms, cafeteria—to name a few. Each construction or renovation was a search for excellence and an effort to meet the integral needs of the students of the day. These improvements to the physical plant were a symbol of the AMC commitment to the educational tradition of the Sisters of Saint Anne: to educate the whole person. This tradition continues to be passed on from generation to generation of students, trustees, chaplains, and lecturers. I know. I have been a student, lecturer, chaplain, and trustee of Anna Maria College and I am proud of our educational heritage.
>
> *— Yvette Bellerose, S.S.A., General Superior of the Sisters of Saint Anne, 1986-1998*

The party turned out to be a reunion of alumnae through the years. Laughter, warmth, and genuine affection were palpable! Stories were told, anecdotes recounted, and laughs shared.

A spectacular event: "A Madrigal Feast" was presented by the music department, under the direction of Professor Mary Lynn Ritchey, at the Castle Restaurant in Leicester. The Anna Maria College chorus and Bel Canto (a small group of singers reminiscent of the Paxtonettes of earlier days) presented Renaissance music from English, Italian, French, and German traditions. The guests were welcomed by King Pomposo Grosso; his Queen, Diva Furiosa; their daughter, Princess Grace, the Amazing; and the entire Royal Court of Collegium Annae Mariae, on the anniversary of the 50th year of its founding, April 1996. The vocal presentations lasting throughout the dinner were impressive, brilliantly rendered, and appreciated by an enthusiastic audience.[98]

In April 1996, Dr. Dill wrote to the friends of Anna Maria College inviting them to celebrate the Golden Anniversary Year by joining the campus community for commencement ceremonies on May 19, 1996. His letter read as follows:

...This is a very special year in the life of Anna Maria College. It was fifty years ago that the Sisters of Saint Anne founded this institution, dedicated to helping women of modest means obtain a college education. Today, AMC has grown into a co-educational institution with over 1800 full- and part-time students studying for undergraduate and graduate degrees. The past fifty years have seen many changes in both the physical and educational aspects of AMC, and now the college is strongly positioned to enter the next century.

The technological infrastructure of the college has been put in place, and we are beginning to establish databases and link offices. Perhaps we have been out of touch with you for awhile, but are attempting to re-establish contact with our many friends, past trustees, donors, and past honorary degree recipients. We would like you to become re-acquainted with the college, and this golden anniversary year is a good time for us to get together again....

On May 19, 1996, graduation day, Liz Walker, news anchor for Channel 4 TV in Boston, received an honorary degree and delivered the main commencement address. There were other honorary degree recipients among whom was Elaine Walter, who received a Bachelor of Music degree from AMC in 1959. She became the first alumna of the undergraduate division to be honored by her Alma Mater. She was serving as dean of the Benjamin T. Rome School of Music at the Catholic University of America and certainly deserved the honor bestowed upon her.[99] It was a red-letter day for her and her family, who were in attendance for the occasion. On Thursday, June 13,

Dr. Bernard S. Parker, seventh president of Anna Maria College.

1996, the Worcester Area Chamber of Commerce "Breakfast Club" honored Anna Maria College on the occasion of its 50th Anniversary. The breakfast, held at Assumption College, was very well attended by representatives from the academic and business communities of Worcester. President Dill accepted a plaque from the Club congratulating the college on its achievements through the last fifty years. Each attendee received a memento of AMC—a cobalt blue mug bearing the AMC seal and a quotation from Thomas Carlyle. It also contained a packet of seeds and a certificate of "seed money" for a theater production at the Zecco

---

DIMENSIONS OF EMERGENCY PLANNING AND RESPONSE

*T*he mission of Anna Maria College includes a commitment to nurturing a sense of responsibility to society and the world. In keeping with this obligation, the graduate department of biological studies, in the late eighties, undertook a serious study of occupational and environmental health and safety measures and sought the services of faculty experts in the field. In the early nineties, Dr. Lorraine Popowicz, chairperson of the department, introduced the Master of Science in Occupational and Environmental Safety. As a sequel to this attractive program, I presented for approval the Master of Science in Emergency Planning and Response, a syllabus with a new thrust but directly complementary to the earlier offering. It includes more than a series of how-to courses; it exposes the student to the recognition that any incident, whether a hurricane or a bombing, an accidental release of toxic industrial gases or purposeful contamination of essential resources can be easily magnified in its toll of human life by the very way we conduct our lives and structure our societies.

Essentially, it was to provide emergency planners in government and industry with a comprehensive and holistic education regarding all dimensions of emergency planning and response as well as of occupational and environmental safety measures that Anna Maria College inaugurated these two very relevant and needed programs.

— *Paul A. Erickson, Ph.D., Associate Professor of biology and natural sciences*

Performing Arts Center. On June 20, Anna Maria College hosted the 1996 MBA Awards Dinner to recognize the outstanding achievements of students, alumni, and faculty of the Anna Maria College MBA program. Champagne and hors d'oeuvres refreshed some 100 MBA enthusiasts, faculty, and friends before dinner and the awards ceremony. Inspired by the events of the anniversary year, President Dill delivered a solid message of hope to those attending emphasizing the value of celebration in the lives of people. Raymond C. Guillette, director of business programs, explained the meaning of each award and presented the recipients who received their award from President Dill, who himself was honored with the Mother Teresa of India Award for leadership and commitment to community service.[100]

July 1, 1996, marked the beginning of Dr. Bernard Parker's tenure as seventh president of Anna Maria College. Dr. Parker spent the summer months familiarizing himself with and adapting to the culture of AMC. Mary Kilcoyne negotiated with *The Catholic Free Press* for a supplement to be produced as part of the college's 50th Anniversary celebration. It appeared on August 30, 1996.[101] The individual articles revealed an interesting tale—the AMC story—which started with a dream and a vision, a story with triumphs and challenges, but especially a story of people inspired and driven by a mission.[102] The supplement was distributed to the entire readership of the diocesan paper and raised the awareness of AMC for hundreds of people. A golden jubilee gala was planned for October 4, 5, and 6, 1996.[103] Alumni, friends, and the entire college community were invited to celebrate the history and the prosperity of Anna Maria College with a weekend full of activities appealing to people of all ages.

*On the occasion of the Golden Jubilee of Anna Maria College,
Sisters Therese Noury and Michele Jacques, co-leaders of St. Marie
Province, gifted the college with a "grand-sister" clock.
Sister Paulette Gardner '67 sets the time.*

piece orchestra, complete with three female vocalists, performed popular music from the 1940s through the 1990s. Both the champagne reception and the dinner dance were held in the Fuller Activities Center.

Sunday, October 6, 1996, was a time to celebrate together. The congregation of the Sisters of Saint Anne and their guests gathered for a special Sunday morning breakfast before the Liturgy. There were presentations to recognize the former presidents assembled for the occasion: Sisters Irene Socquet, Bernadette Madore, and Rita Larivee. Members who had been part of the AMC campus community since 1952 were also honored: Sister Irene Socquet, Sister Clarice Chauvin, Sister Lorraine Plette, and Sister Bernadette Madore. Sister Bernadette spent some moments presenting the highlights of the college's history from 1946 to 1996. The assembly, made up of many sisters who themselves lived the history in varied ways, was attentive and the smiles betrayed the joy and interest of all present.

At 12:00 noon, in the Zecco Performing Arts Center, Bishop George E. Rueger celebrated the Eucharist during which Dr. Bernard S. Parker was commissioned as seventh president of Anna Maria College. It was a memorable event and the first time that a President of AMC was so installed. Immediately following this event, the assembly gathered in the Mondor-Eagen Library where Sister Therese Noury and Sister Michele Jacques, provincial leaders of the Sisters of Saint Anne, presented a fiftieth anniversary "grand-sister" clock to grace the entrance to the library and to commemorate the golden anniversary of the college. The final weekend celebration was a gala luncheon full of good

Highlights of the weekend program included a presentation by Robert V. Antonucci, Massachusetts Commissioner of Education, to celebrate AMC's fifty years of excellence in education. More than twenty art-alumni participated in an alumni art exhibit in St. Luke's Gallery at the Moll Art Center.

On Saturday, October 5, 1996, the festival included a medley of activities to suit every age and fancy. A Latin dance troupe, antique vehicles, hay rides, museum displays, strolling musicians were just a few of the many exhibitions, demonstrations, entertainments, special events, and fun activities highlighting the AMC story throughout the Paxton campus. On the same day, a memorable event occurred—the unveiling of AMC's internet web site produced in its final form by Sister Rita Larivee, former president of AMC. Joe Kane, one of the technicians had contributed to the earlier production phases. On Saturday evening, a champagne reception was the prelude to the anniversary alumni reunion featuring a jubilee dinner with dance. The ten-

cheer for the past and hope for the future.

On November 16, 1996, Dr. Bernard S. Parker invited special guests to the 1996 President's Club and Council dinner. The reception began at 6:00 P.M. and dinner was served at 7:00. Reminders of the Golden Anniversary were present everywhere; as part of the menu, in the speeches, and in the good cheer which permeated the audience. The classical guitar of Peter Clemente and the legendary Bel Canto of Anna Maria College entertained the guests in a brilliant performance. It was Anna Maria's way of expressing thanks for the friendship and support of all present.

From October 27 to November 23, Anna Maria College presented artistic expressions of the Sisters of Saint Anne, an exhibition in conjunction with the celebration of their 100th anniversary as an incorporated province. The exhibit was held in St. Luke's Gallery of the Moll Art Center.

To end the Golden Anniversary year for Anna Maria College, the alumni were challenged to raise a total of $50,000 in the last 50 calendar days. Generous friends came forward with the idea of matching every dollar raised by December 31, 1996. Thanks to the jump start, the mini-campaign raised $82,780—a total of $32,780 beyond the goal of $50,000! Nineteen ninety-six was a year of grace for the college. The dream and the vision were real. A mission inspired the initiative of 1946 and this mission evolved with changing times. To educate remains the cornerstone of the enterprise but this aim is approached and pursued in ways appropriate to the needs of the time and the voids to be filled.

Anna Maria's success in the past and the present was directly linked to the willingness to see new opportunities and pursue them.

XVIII

POSTLUDE
1946-1996

In 1946, Anna Maria College was a small, undergraduate women's institution. Its mission was to provide a solid liberal arts education to women of modest means. Programs of concentration (majors) were in art, biology, chemistry, education, English, French, history, music, and sociology. There were required basic courses in philosophy, religion, French/Spanish/German, mathematics/Greek/Latin, history, and speech. Other courses such as physics and economics were requirements for certain fields of concentration. This comparative simplicity of curriculum was considered a strength rather than a weakness. The faculty, most of them Sisters of Saint Anne, were experienced and well prepared. Several were administrators and part-time professors simultaneously. All of them were enthusiastic and dedicated. They knew the students well and were attentive to their individual needs.

Most of the students were Catholic women from Worcester county who looked forward to marriage and motherhood, and they regarded a liberal arts education as a training of the intellect that would enhance their domestic future. Classes were small, teaching was excellent, and extra-curricular experiences plentiful and valuable. To graduate, the student needed to earn 132 credits including sixteen in religion and eighteen in philosophy, pass the modern language examination, the comprehensive examination in the field of concentration, and take the graduate record examination. In 1959, 46 percent of those who obtained a bachelor's degree did some graduate work. The physical plant was adequate for the needs of this small population of students; but, as their number grew, there would be need for more library space. In 1959, services donated by the sisters could be considered as the equivalent of a substantial endowment.

The seventies and eighties produced their own challenges regarding the future of higher education. Undergraduate students were in short supply and the mortality rate of small, liberal arts institutions was high; federal and state monies

185

THE NEW MILLENNIUM

William D. McGarry, eighth president of Anna Maria College.

The millennial year, which saw the publication of this history also marked the inauguration of Anna Maria College's eighth president, William D. McGarry. This new leader brings great promise and a strong sense of stability to the college. His inauguration was held at St. Paul's Cathedral in the presence of the entire college community—trustees, students, staff, and faculty joined with alumni, friends, former trustees, and administrators—all of whom, over the years, helped Anna Maria College to grow. The reception following the cathedral ceremony was at the renovated Union Station, sparkling in its attractive newness.

the excellence of Anna Maria could not be limited to the past. They willingly exchanged the *modus operandi* of the fifties and sixties for a more comprehensive sense of direction; even the mission statement evolved and reflected what Anna Maria was gradually becoming. The power of hope played a vital role as the institution committed itself to the dynamism of the future. For administrators and faculty, there was an urgent need to develop a new vision for the college and create its future. To them, the future sometimes took on the qualities of a mirage—always moving, always elusive. Still, they were convinced that success could be achieved, not suddenly, but by determined effort, one day at a time.

for educational programs were cut back or eliminated. It was a question of survival. For Anna Maria College, one of the key responses to the crisis was to seek and provide education for non-traditional students. It was also crucial in this period of survival and growth—especially in the eighties—to confront the academic community with a fast-moving, information-oriented society.

By 1974, institutional diversification had brought new vitality to Anna Maria College. The college was no longer a small, day-time, undergraduate women's institution. Academic programs tripled, the college was co-educational, had a graduate division, with hundreds of nontraditional students and off-campus sites. Experimental teaching and new administrative approaches enlarged the traditional population, enriched values, and enhanced the ethos of the college. The mission of Anna Maria College continued to reflect the heritage of the early institution; it also included a dynamic direction for growth. While several of its sister institutions disappeared, victims of statistical reality, Anna Maria not only survived but prospered and grew. Faculty and administrators became aware that

STABILITY VERSUS FLEXIBILITY

I recently found myself teaching the offspring of a former student, an experience with several layers of meaning. A significant number of others also have served here that long, which demonstrates our stability. And the fact that children of graduates come here for the kind of education we have always offered, professional and liberal education embedded in a Catholic context, illustrates the power of tradition. The student to whom I refer, however, is male and he is enrolled in a program that did not exist during his mother's stay at AMC, when we were still a women's college; not everything has remained as it was. We are an institution where stability and tradition coexist with flexibility and growth. The more we change, the more we remain the same, and that is as it should be.

— *Dr. Robert H. Goepfert, Professor of music*

Greater legislative demands regarding student life, a drug-free environment, the reporting of crime, and greater security affected higher education across the land. The task at hand in dealing with these issues was to maintain a clear grasp of the college's vision. American culture was changing and new cultures were introduced as large numbers of immigrants from many lands sought their place in the fabric of the nation. The college needed to be attuned to these significant changes and trends as well as be able to respond to them with responsibility and

A CATHOLIC LIBERAL ARTS COLLEGE

... *W*hat we have been given is a Catholic liberal arts college—if we can keep it! Keeping it has not been such an easy task to date; nor does it promise to get any easier. Many people whom we could have legitimately expected to support us have simply not done so; they have remained on the sidelines. As long as the Sisters of Saint Anne were numerous, it did not matter all that much. The Sisters were able to build this campus by donating their services, returning what otherwise would have been their salaries to the general fund. And when it came time to do something special, like move the library, they simply carried the books.

— *Robert J. Lemieux, Professor of philosophy and French*

Sisters of St. Anne moving books to the library in July 1963.
This picture was used in one of Anna Maria College's first fundraising pieces with the caption, "We have always been big on doing it ourselves, now we realize we need your help." The picture later appeared in Time Magazine.

maturity, always in light of its early mission. All academic trends indicated a dramatic shift in the economic system causing an even greater impact than that which occurred when the nation shifted from an agricultural to an industrial nation. There was need for a new holistic vision of education for the nineties and beyond, consistent with present realities. Anna Maria's success in the past and the present was directly linked to its willingness to see new opportunities and pursue them. It needed to remain vital and dynamic. The nation relied on higher education to maintain a competitive stance in the world arena.

As a small, privately-supported, religiously-affiliated institution, Anna Maria College has emphasized not only the liberal arts and sciences but also solid training for professional careers. The college's size and its flexibility in maintaining a distinctive mission, its emphasis on teaching excellence, its personalized approach to all student needs, and its willingness to act swiftly and creatively—these were the determining factors in recognizing opportunities and pursuing them successfully.

The hope at Anna Maria is that morality and spirituality will always be familiar and accepted benchmarks; that idealism will never be an embarrassment; that the college will continue to stand out from the crowd, be true to lofty ideals, and achieve quality in every possible way.

Faculty and administrators have realized that the future is not a place; it is what the college is always becoming, first in imagination and vision, next in thought and plan, and finally in action. The future of Anna Maria is a unique creation carved out of the choices it makes and the values it keeps adding to its accomplishments. To fuel its vitality and sustain its relevance, it will always need the vigor, the dynamism, and the generous support of its alumni who represent Anna Maria College wherever they are.

AD MULTOS ANNOS!

THE AUTHOR'S CONCLUDING REMARKS

The history of Anna Maria College reflects in many ways the parable of the mustard seed. At the end of World War II, we, the Sisters of St. Anne, began as pioneers in the Archdiocese of Boston. Then with great faith and energy, we established the present campus in Paxton, in the Diocese of Worcester. We faced formidable challenges and won formidable victories. Through the great impetus coming from our congregation, we not only grew, but we also prospered. We built a beautiful campus and an important institution. In so doing, we served not only thousands of students ranging in age from the late teens to the advanced sixties, but also the broader community without ever losing sight of our mission.

With the dawn of the third millennium, major events emphasized new beginnings both for the college and the sponsoring congregation, the Sisters of Saint Anne.

President McGarry's inauguration was by far the major event of the jubilee year for Anna Maria College. For the Sisters of Saint Anne, the millennium brought a tapestry of great moments of which every thread was and is being cherished. The celebration of the 150th anniversary of the congregation and the coming beatification of Venerable Mother Marie Anne, its foundress, were the major events which provided a rich background for the numerous celebrations.

In anticipation of this unforgettable year, Anna Maria College, from April 11-25, 1999, proudly presented a century of artistic zeal and passion. The selected paintings depicted a variety of religious subject matter, landscapes, still lifes, and portraits in a number of styles and artistic mediums. Choices were made from the work of several Sisters who were trained by European artists in the late 19th century and into the 20th century, even as the Sisters instructed students of their own.

The millennium year continues to be a beautiful one for every Sister of Saint Anne and also for Anna Maria College. Because the college is an apostolate created by the congregation, it has been given a proud place in this panoply of events.

*Two works featured in the exhibit "A Sacred Passion: The Art of
the Sisters of Saint Anne."
Above:* **The Holy Family,** *by Sr. M. Helene-de-la-Croix,
oil on canvas, 58" x 48".
Right:* **Child in a White Apron,** *by Sr. M. Helene-de-la-Croix,
oil on canvas, 27" x 21".*

Presidents of Anna Maria College

Sister M. Anne Eva Mondor, S.S.A.	1946-1951
Sister Irene Marie Socquet, S.S.A.	1951-1975
Sister Caroline Finn, S.S.A.	1975-1977
Sister Bernadette Madore, S.S.A.	1977-1993
Sister Rita Larivee, S.S.A.	1993-1994
William R. Dill, Ph.D.	1995-1996
Bernard S. Parker, Ph.D.	1996-1999
William D. McGarry	1999-

Provincial Superiors of St. Marie Province
1945 - 2000

Sister M. Jean Cassien, S.S.A.	1945-1951
Sister M. Louise Ida, S.S.A.	1951-1957
Sister M. Pauline Therese, S.S.A.	1957-1963
Sister Blanche Morency, S.S.A.	1963-1969
Sister M. George Edmond, S.S.A.	1969-1973
Sister Lorraine Marie, S.S.A.	1973-1979
Sister Constance Gosselin, S.S.A.	1979-1984
Sister Therese Dion, S.S.A.	1984-1987
Sister Jeannette Robichaud, S.S.A.	1987-1993
Sisters Therese Noury and Michele Jacques, S.S.A.	1993-1999
Sisters Yvette Dargy and Paulette Gardner, S.S.A.	1999-

On April 13, 1980, a predominantly lay Board of Trustees was established. The following is a list of members who have served on the Board :

Abdella, Charles, A., J.D.
Andreoli, Arthur J.
Audette, Muriel, S.S.A.
Babin, Doris, S.SA.
Baehrecke, Christian
Baker, Dennis J.
Bassett, Edward C., J.D.
Bayeur, Constance, S.S.A.
Bellerose, Yvette, S.S.A.
Bernstein, William E., J.D.
Bibeau, Annette, S.S.A.
Blute, Peter
Breault, Arthur
Brooks, John E., S.J., Ph.D.
Caparso, Richard C.
Caparso-Limoges, Marie U., Ph.D.
Chand, Ronald H.
Chasse, Diane, S.S.A.
Cocaine, Mary T.
Coghlin, Maureen L.
Coogan, Michael, CFRE
Cosgrove, James, J.D.
Dargy, Yvette, S.S.A.
DeRoy, Rita, S.S.A.
Dill, William, R., Ph.D.
Dumas, Paul A., M.D.
Early, Thomas J. *
Ferrante, Ellen
Flanagan, Bishop Bernard J., D.D. *
Flynn, Barbara, S.S.A.
Foley, Daniel J.
Freelander, I. Robert
Gadoury, Rose Clarisse, S.S.A.

Gagnon, Doris M., S.S.A.
Gardner, Paulette, S.S.A.
Gatto, Michele S., J.D.
Guerin, William V
Harrington, Daniel, J.
Hasso, Mark H.
Hedge, James E. *
Helfenbein, Gerald J. *
Hennessey, Mary, R.C. *
Hogan, Robert J.
Hourihan, Thomas J.
Jacobsen, Julia
Jacques, Elise A., M.D.
Jefferson, Mildred D., M.D
Kane, Kevin H..
Kehoe, John F., J.D.
Kelleher, William D.
Keller, Anthony J.
Kelly, Suzanne C.
Kelly, Monsignor Francis J.
Larivee, Rita, S.S.A., Ph.D.
Laurence, Pauline, S.S.A.
Lauring, Mark
Lazare, Aaron, M.D.
LeBoeuf, Jacqueline, S.S.A.
Levenson, Harry *
Macpherson, David M.
Madore, Bernadette, S.S.A., Ph.D.
Maguire, Shirley M.
Mahoney, Colleen, S.S.A.
McGarry, William D.
McKenney, James
McMullen, Cynthia M.

McNamara, Richard B.
Mercandante, Louis P.
Murphy, Msgr. John F., S.T.D.
Nolder, Barbara
Noury, Therese, S.S.A.
O'Coin, Robert E. *
O'Coin, Eleanor
O'Leary, Cornelius J.
Ouellette, Lucille A., Ph.D.
Parker, Bernard S., Ph.D.
Podbielski, Joseph, M.D. *
Proietti, Carol, S.S.A.
Prunier, J. Edward, M.D.
Purcell, Alfred J.
Quinn, Mary Ann, S.S.A.
Rabbitt, Joseph E.
Race, Candace A.
Richard, Christine M., S.S.A.
Robichaud, Jeannette, S.S.A.
Rueger, Bishop George E.
Simonds, Janet C.
Sokol, Thomas P.*
Tasse, M. Jeanne, Ph.D.
Tinsley, Msgr. Edmond
Tomlinson, Joseph *
Walker, Kathleen
Walter, Elaine, M., Ph.D.
Waniewski, Eugene C.
White, Thomas P.
Williams,Robert F.,M.D.
Woods, William
Zecco, Patrick

*deceased
list as of 3/28/00

REFERENCES

Anna Maria College. 50th Anniversary. A Supplement of *The Catholic Free Press*. August 30, 1996.

A Task Force on the Search for Excellence. AMC archives. Paxton, MA.

Anna Maria College Catalog. 1948. AMC archives. Paxton, MA.

Bock, Sister M. Liliane, SSA. Correspondence. SSA archives. Lachine, Quebec.

Chronicles of the Sisters of Saint Anne in Paxton. SSA archives. Paxton, MA.

Cushing, Richard, J. Correspondence. SSA archives. Lachine, Quebec.

Deferrari, Roy. Correspondence. SSA archives, Lachine, Quebec.

Duggan, Joseph, C. Correspondence. SSA archives. Lachine, Quebec.

Eagen, Sister M. Rose Isabel, SSA. Personal notes. SSA archives. Marlboro, MA.

Finn, Caroline, S.S.A. Annual Reports of the President to the Board of Trustees. SSA and AMC archives. Paxton, MA.

Freedman, Leonard. ed. Issues of the Sixties. Sec. ed. 1965-1970. Belmont, CA: Wadsworth Publishing Co. 1965.

Gallagher, Buell G. Campus In Crisis. New York, NY: Harper & Row. 1974.

John Paul II. *Ex Corde Ecclesiae*. Apostolic Constitution on Catholic Higher Education. Rome. August 15, 1990.

L'Ecuyer, Sister M. Leopoldine, SSA. Correspondence. SSA archives. Lachine, Quebec.

Madore, Bernadette, SSA. Annual Reports of the President to the Board of Trustees. SSA and AMC archives. Paxton, MA.

Madore, Bernadette, SSA. Annual Reports of the Dean of the College to the President. SSA and. AMC archives. Paxton, MA.

Madore, Bernadette, SSA. Letters from the President in issues of *Milestone*. AMC archives. Paxton, MA.

Mazzaglia, Francis, R. The Case Study of a Catholic College Which Overcame Adversity: Anna Maria College 1965-1985. Diss. Harvard U. 1989.

Meloche, Sister M. Jean Cassien, SSA. Correspondence. SSA archives. Lachine, Quebec.

Meetings of the Advisory Board of Anna Maria College. Minutes. AMC archives. Paxton, MA.

Meetings of the Faculty of Anna Maria College. Minutes. AMC archives. Paxton, MA.

Meetings of the Officers of Anna Maria College. Minutes. AMC archives. Paxton, MA.

Miller, Douglas, T. Visions of America. New York:West Publishing Co. 1988.

Mondor, Sister M. Anne Eva, SSA. Correspondence. SSA archives. Lachine, Quebec.

National Catholic Educational Association. Report. SSA archives. Lachine, Quebec.

New England Association of Schools and Colleges. Reports. AMC archives. Paxton, MA.

Price, John. Notes. AMC archives. Paxton, MA.

Proceedings Concerning Anna Maria College Legislation. Report. SSA archives. Lachine,Quebec.

Roy, Louise, SSA. *Les Soeurs de Sainte-Anne*. Tome II (1900-1950). 1992.

Sixteenth General Chapter of the Sisters of Saint Anne.Article 13. SSA archives. Lachine, Quebec.

Smelser, Marshall & Joan R. Gunderson. <u>American History at a Glance</u>. 4th ed. New York: Barnes and Noble Books. 1978.

Socquet, Irene, SSA. Correspondence. SSA archives. Lachine, Quebec.

Socquet, Irene, SSA. Annual Reports of the President to the Board of Trustees. SSA and AMC archives. Paxton, MA.

Soldani, Louise. Annual Reports of the Dean of the College to the President. AMC archives. Paxton, MA.

Sullivan, T.D. Correspondence. SSA archives. Lachine, Quebec.

The Corporation of the Sisters of St. Ann. Minutes. SSA archives. Paxton, MA.

The Comerford Estate. Report. SSA archives. Lachine, Quebec.

The General Council of the Sisters of Saint Anne. Minutes. SSA archives. Lachine, Quebec.

United States Department of Education. Title III. Correspondence. AMC archives. Paxton, MA.

Wright, John J. Correspondence. SSA archives. Lachine, Quebec.

ENDNOTES

1. Sister M. Jean-de-Pathmos, S.S.A., *Les Soeurs de Sainte-Anne: Un Siecle d'Histoire*, Tome I, 1850-1900 (Lachine: SSA Archives), 11-66.

2. Anita Poudrier, S.S.A., <u>A Tradition Unfolds: The Sisters of Saint Anne in the United States</u> (Lachine: Les Editions Sainte-Anne, 1997), 37;83.

3. Anna Maria College Catalog, 1948 (Paxton: AMC Archives), 7.

4. Louise Roy, S.S.A., *Les Soeurs de Sainte-Anne, Un Siecle d'Histoire*, Tome 2, 1900-1950 (Lachine: SSA Archives), 261-290.

5. Sixteenth General Chapter of the Sisters of Saint Anne (Lachine: SSA Archives), Article 13.

6. Sister M. Rose Isabel Eagen, S.S.A., Personal notes (Marlboro: SSA Archives), 1968.

7. Sister M. Anne Eva Mondor, S.S.A., letter to Mother M. Leopoldine, S.S.A., 6 October 1945 (Lachine: SSA Archives).

8. Mondor, S.S.A., 4 October 1945 (Lachine: SSA Archives).

9. Roy J. Deferrari, letter to Sister M. Anne Eva Mondor, S.S.A., 6 March 1946 (Lachine: SSA Archives).

10. Timothy F. O'Leary, letter to Sister M. Anne Eva Mondor, S.S.A., 4 December 1945 (Lachine: SSA Archives)

11. Mondor, S.S.A., 17 December 1945 (Lachine: SSA Archives).

12. Mother M. Leopoldine, S.S.A., letter to Archbishop Cushing, 24 January 1946 (Lachine: SSA Archives)

13. Archbishop Cushing, letter to Mother M. Leopoldine, S.S.A., 26 January 1946 (Lachine: SSA Archives)

14. Mondor, S.S.A., 26 February 1946 (Lachine: SSA Archives).

15. The expenses suggested were as follows:

For resident students

Tuition	$200.00
Board and residence	$250.00

For non-resident students

Tuition	$200.00
Lunches	$ 75.00

For all students

Registration (payable once)	$10.00
Library fee	$10.00
Laboratory fee	$15.00
Special examination	$ 2.00
Board during college recess	$ 1.00/day

16. Mondor, S.S.A., letter to Timothy O'Leary, 7 March 1946 (Lachine: SSA Archives).

17. Archbishop Cushing, letter to Joseph Duggan, 18 April 1946 (Lachine: SSA Archives).

18. Joseph Duggan, letter to Sister M. Anne Eva Mondor, S.S.A., 7 May 1946 (Lachine: SSA Archives).

19. Mondor, S.S.A., letter to general superior, 30 April 1947 (Lachine: SSA Archives).

20. Mondor, S.S.A., letter to Mother M. Leopoldine, S.S.A., 21 May 1948 (Lachine: SSA

Archives).

21. Minutes of faculty meetings, 12 January 1947 and 15 October 1949 (Paxton: AMC Archives).

22. T. D. Sullivan, report to the committee on membership of the National Catholic Educational Association, 1 December 1950 (Lachine: SSA Archives).

23. Roy, S.S.A., 233-234, 429 (Lachine: SSA Archives).

24. Mondor, S.S.A., letter to Mother M. Liliane, S.S.A., 5 January 1951 (Lachine: SSA Archives).

25. Mondor, S.S.A., report on the Comerford Estate to Mother M. Leopoldine, S.S.A., 7 July 1950 (Lachine: SSA Archives).

26 O'Leary, letter to Sister M. Anne Eva Mondor, S.S.A., 10 August 1950 (Lachine: SSA Archives).

27. Mother M. Liliane, S.S.A., letter to Archbishop Cushing, 5 May 1951 (Lachine: SSA Archives).

28. Mother M. Liliane, S.S.A., letter to Bishop Wright, 11 May 1951 (Lachine: SSA Archives)

29. Bishop John J. Wright, letter to Mother M. Liliane, S.S.A., 14 May 1951 (Lachine: SSA Archives).

30. Sister M. Jean-de-Pathmos, S.S.A., 392 (Lachine: SSA Archives).

31. Chronicles of the Sisters of Saint Anne in Paxton, 31 May 1951 (Paxton: SSA Archives).

32. Eagen, S.S.A., personal notes (Marlboro: SSA Archives).

33. Chronicles of the Sisters of Saint Anne in Paxton, 1952-1953 (Paxton: SSA Archives)

34. Minutes of a meeting of the corporation *The Sisters of St. Ann*, 2 September 1952 (Marlboro: SSA Archives)

35. *Annales de la Communaute des Soeurs de Sainte-Anne*, January 1953 (Lachine: SSA Archives).

36. Minutes of a meeting of the local council of the Sisters of Saint Anne, 12 February 1959 (Paxton: SSA Archives). Laurence Cournoyer and Raymond Paulin, conversation with author, November 1998.

37. Nils Y. Wessell, letter to Sister Irene Socquet, S.S.A., 10 December 1953 (Paxton: AMC Archives).

38. Wessell, letter to Sister Irene Socquet, S.S.A., 14 January 1954 (Paxton: AMC Archives).

39. Meribeth E. Cameron, report to the New England Association of Schools and Colleges, 1955 (Paxton: AMC Archives).

40. Dana M. Cotton, letter to Sister Irene Socquet, S.S.A., 15 December 1955 (Paxton: AMC Archives).

41. Socquet, S.S.A., letter to Sister M. Anne Eva Mondor, S.S.A., 17 December 1955 (Lachine: SSA Archives).

42. Eagen, S.S.A., personal notes (Marlboro: SSA Archives).

43. Acts of the local SSA council in Paxton, 1951-1952 (Paxton: SSA Archives).

44. Minutes of a meeting of the corporation, *The Sisters of St. Ann*, 21 July 1958 (Marlboro: SSA Archives).

45. Socquet, S.S.A., annual report to the board of trustees, 1964-1965 (Paxton: SSA and AMC Archives).

46. Cardinal Cushing Hall construction cost: $307, 560; cost/square foot: $17.08; total cost including furnishings, $390, 254; $21.68/square foot (Paxton: AMC Archives).

47. W.H. Taylor, letter to Sister Irene Socquet, S.S.A., 2 March 1963 (Paxton: AMC Archives).

48. Douglas T. Miller, <u>Visions of America</u> (New York: West Publishing Co. 1988), 229.

49. Miller, 227.

50. Marshall Smelser and Joan R. Gunderson, <u>American History At A Glance</u> (New York: Harper and Row, 1978), 253.

51. Francis R. Mazzaglia, <u>The Case Study of a Catholic College Which Overcame Adversity</u> (Diss. Harvard U.) 1989.

52. Minutes of a meeting of the corporation *The Sisters of St. Ann*, 28 June 1972 (Marlboro: SSA Archives).

53. Minutes of a meeting of the corporation *The Sisters of St. Ann*, 13 September 1974 (Marlboro: SSA Archives).

54. Cyhthia Taylor, letter to Sister Irene Socquet, S.S.A., 1975 (Paxton: SSA Archives).

55. Buell G. Gallagher, <u>Campus in Crisis</u> (New York: Harper and Row, 1974).

56. Minutes of a meeting of the corporation *The Sisters of St. Ann*, 18 February 1975 (Marlboro: SSA Archives).

57. Sister Caroline Finn, S.S.A., annual report to the board of trustees, 1975-1976 (Paxton: AMC Archives).

58. Minutes of a meeting of the corporation *The Sisters of St. Ann*, 3 June 1977 (Marlboro: SSA Archives).

59. Minutes of a meeting of the corporation *The Sisters of St. Ann*, 16 June 1978 (Marlboro: SSA Archives).

60. Minutes of a meeting of the corporation *The Sisters of St. Ann*, 29 June 1978 (Marlboro: SSA Archives).

61. Harold L. Hodgkinson, <u>Guess Who's Coming to College: Your Students in 1990</u> (Washington, D.C. National Institute of Independent Colleges and Universities, 1983), 5-9.

62. Minutes of a meeting of the corporation *The Sisters of St. Ann*, 8 October 1973 (Marlboro: SSA Archives).

63. Minutes of a meeting of the corporation *The Sisters of St. Ann*, 24 June 1974 (Marlboro: SSA Archives).

64. Minutes of meetings of the corporation T*he Sisters of St. Ann*, 9, 17 November 1973; 8 March 1974, 3 May 1974, 14 June 1974 (Marlboro: SSA Archives).

65. Minutes of a meeting of the corporation *The Sisters of St. Ann*, 24 June 1974 (Marlboro: SSA Archives).

66. Ibid.

67. Roland V. Stoodley, letter to Sister Bernadette Madore, S.S.A., 10 May 1979 (Paxton: AMC Archives).

68. Minutes of meetings of the corporation *The Sisters of St. Ann*, 1,2,3 June 1976; 31 January, 28 March 1977, 9 February, 11, 16 March, 3, 30 May, 28 June, 30 July, 1 September, 12 October, 9 November, 14 December 1979; 25 January, 27 March, 11 April 1980 (Marlboro: SSA Archives).

69. New England Association of Schools and Colleges, evaluation report, November 1978 (Paxton: AMC Archives).

70. Minutes of a meeting of the corporation *The Sisters of St. Ann*, 28 June 1979 (Marlboro: SSA Archives)

71. Minutes of meetings of the corporation *The Sisters of St. Ann*, 30 July and 9 November 1979 (Marlboro: SSA Archives).

72. Minutes of a meeting of the corporation *The Sisters of St. Ann* 28 September 1979 (Marlboro: SSA Archives).

73. Minutes of meetings of the board of trustees, 27 March and 11 April 1980 (Marlboro: SSA Archives).

74. Department of Education, Washington, D.C., notification of grant award for Title III, 27

September 1982 (Paxton: AMC Archives).

75. Total cost of the construction of Mondor-Eagen Library was $909,578. This did not include the cost of furniture and equipment amounting to $91,605.

76. Sister Bernadette Madore, S.S.A., Annual Reports of the President, 1983-1984, 1884-1985 (Paxton: AMC Archives).

77. Madore, S.S.A., Annual Report of the President, 1984-1985 (Paxton: AMC Archives).

78. Madore, S.S.A., Annual Reports of the President, 1983-1984; 1984-1985 (Paxton: AMC Archives).

79. Madore, S.S.A., Annual Report of the President, 1985-1986 (Paxton: AMC Archives). The names of the four sisters were: Sisters Irene Socquet, Clarice Chauvin, Lorraine Plette, Bernadette Madore, S.S.A.

80. Madore, S.S.A. Annual Report of the President, 1987-1988 (Paxton: AMC Archives).

81. Paul Reiss, report to the New England Association of Schools and Colleges, 1988 (Paxton: AMC Archives).

82. Madore, S.S.A., Annual Reports of the President, 1984-1988 (Paxton: AMC Archives).

83. "AMCats Claw Their Way To a NCAA Sweet 16", *Visions*, Spring 1996, 8-14 (Paxton: AMC Archives).

84. Long-Range Plans for 1988-1992, January 1988 (Paxton: AMC Archives).

85. Madore, S.S.A., Annual Report of the President, 1989-1990 (Paxton: AMC Archives).

86. Ibid.

87. Richard Duckett, *Worcester Telegram and Gazette Date Book*, 26 December 1993.

88. Mo Fung, "Bishops Wrestle Over Document On Catholic Colleges and Universities", *The Pilot*, 28 June 1996, 18 (Paxton: AMC Archives).

89. Madore, S.S.A., Annual Report of the President, 1991-1992 (Paxton: AMC Archives).

90. Walter Noyalis, report on discussions of *Ex Corde Ecclesiae*, 1993 (Paxton: AMC Archives).

91. Madore, S.S.A., Annual Report of the President, 1991-1992 (Paxton: AMC Archives).

92. Ibid, 4.

93. Minutes of meetings of the executive committee of the board of trustees, 1991-1996 (Paxton: AMC Archives).

94. "AMC Trustees Select Next President," *Visions*, Spring 1996, 16 (Paxton: AMC Archives).

95. Madore, S.S.A., Annual Report of the President, 1991-1992, 10 (Paxton: AMC Archives).

96. John Price, notes to the author, 1997. (Paxton: SSA Archives).

97. "AMC Nurses Making a Difference in Lithuania," *Visions*, Spring 1996 (Paxton: AMC Archives).

98. "Money Guide Ranks AMC number 18," *Visions*, September 1995 (Paxton: AMC Archives). *Money Guide* is among two or three most highly regarded of national efforts to compare and rank colleges.

99. "A Madrigal Feast," *Visions*, Summer 1996, 8-14 (Paxton: AMC Archives).

100. Ibid., 4-5.

101. Ibid., 16.

102. "Anna Maria College — 50th Anniversary, " A Supplement of *The Catholic Free Press*, 30 August 1996 (Paxton: AMC Archives).

103. "Golden Jubilee Gala," Program, 4,5,6 October 1996 (Paxton: AMC Archives).